NEIL HODGSON
Back on track

NEIL HODGSON
Back on Track

NEIL HODGSON
with NEIL BRAMWELL

CollinsWillow

An Imprint of HarperCollins*Publishers*

First published in Great Britain in 2001
by CollinsWillow
an imprint of HarperCollins*Publishers* London

Copyright © Neil Hodgson and Neil Bramwell 2001

3 5 7 9 8 6 4 2

A CIP catalogue record for this book is
available from the British Library

The HarperCollins website address is: www.**fire**and**water**.com

ISBN 0 00 712 646 8

Typeset by Mick Sanders

Printed and bound in Great Britain by
Clays Ltd, St Ives plc

PICTURE ACKNOWLEDGEMENTS

Author's own collection p15 bottom right; p16 top right/
Alex Puczyniec p10 top left; p10 bottom; p11 middle; p11 bottom;
p15 top; p15 top right/ **Keith Martin** p8 top; p11 top; p16 top left;
p16 middle left; p16 middle right/ **Kel Edge** p1 bottom; p2 top left;
p2 top right; p3 bottom; p4 top; p4 bottom right; p6 top; p6 middle;
p8 bottom; p9 top left; p9 bottom; p10 top right; p10 middle; p14 bottom;
p15 middle; p15 bottom left/ **Gee•Bee Photographic (Graeme Brown)** p5
middle right; p5 bottom left; p5 bottom right; p7 bottom; p9 middle right;
p12 bottom; p13 top and bottom; p14 top/ **Goldandgoose** p1 top;
p2 bottom; p3 top; p3 middle right; p4 bottom left; p5 top; p6 bottom;
p7 top; p9 top right; p9 middle left; p12 top; p16 bottom

Contents

Acknowledgements   vii

Introduction   ix

Valencia – round 1   1

Kyalami – round 2   20

Phillip Island – round 3   39

Sugo – round 4   61

Monza – round 5   79

Donington – round 6   94

EuroSpeedway Lausitz – round 7   115

Misano – round 8   130

Laguna Seca – round 9   144

Brands Hatch – round 10   160

Oscherleben – round 11   181

Assen – round 12   199

Imola– round 13   215

Round by round results   231

Final standings   233

*To my dad Mark and mum Maureen
for everything they have ever done for me*

Acknowledgements

I would like to thank Kathryn for agreeing to marry me and putting up with me throughout the season; Darrell and Michelle Healey, for making it all possible; Colin Wright and all the GSE Racing team, for all their hard work and much-appreciated support; Roger and Marit Burnett, and everyone at RBP, for their guidance over the past 10 years; and all my personal sponsors: John and Kath Jones at HM Plant, Joe Henderson at Henderson Insurance Brokers, all the gang at Travelworld, Harvie Puaar at Born to be Wild, Phil Jessopp at Riders of Bridgwater, all the gang at Axo (Italy) and Axo (UK), and Donald Mackay at Lexelle. Finally, thanks to Neil Bramwell for all his hard work and for making the writing of this book an enjoyable experience.

Introduction

I trudged back into the Isle of Man flat that I share with my girlfriend Kathryn, with 36 staples in my arm and feeling pretty sorry for myself. It was the end of the 1999 British season, and I had just had an operation to cure the arm pump I'd been suffering with all year. I needed pampering, but Kathryn was away with her job as an airhostess.

I turned into the bedroom to find Flat Eric, whom we'd both adored in the Levi's Jeans adverts, next to a bag of Maltesers and a message that read:

'Hello! My name is Flat Eric and I'm here to look after you while Kathryn is away.'

I was killing myself laughing and he did a great job of keeping me company until Kathryn returned home a few days later. In fact, Flat Eric soon became part of the family – to the extent that we now talk to him as if he's a human being – and travelled to every meeting with us in 2000, when I won the British championship. For someone who had not enjoyed a huge slice of luck in the previous four seasons, he was quickly recognised as something of a lucky charm.

So imagine my dismay when, on arriving at Valencia for this season's final official pre-season test before I made the step up to World Superbikes with the GSE Racing team, I found that Flat

Eric had been left behind on the island. Was it just a coincidence that I had a disaster over those two days? I don't think so, and I know that there is no chance that the mistake will be repeated for the rest of this year. Eric's powers are not to be under-estimated.

We all know that Eric can drive a car – he proved that in the television advert – but to become a fully paid-up member of the Hodgson family, we will have to get him on a bike, for motorbikes are in my blood. My dad, Mark, was always passionate about bikes and did race on the short circuits for about five seasons. But having married at the age of 17, to support my mum, Maureen, my brother Carl and myself in a small house in Nelson, he had to work all the hours God sent in a variety of jobs such as a car mechanic, scrapman and painter and decorator. He could not, therefore, afford to fall off. I started to ride schoolboy motocross from the age of nine along with Carl until, aged 16, I started club racing. I don't think dad was too pleased when mum pointed out, after I won my second club race, that I'd achieved more in two races than he had in five years of competition!

The following year I entered the 125cc British championship, winning it in my second season at the age of 18. From there I spent two seasons riding in 125 GPs before spending a year in 500 GPs for the WCM team. I started one race, the Argentinian Grand Prix, from the front row and finished the top privateer of the season. This was the year that people started to sit up and take notice of my potential.

The next two years were spent as a factory rider for Ducati, with two of the most difficult team-mates imaginable. Both John Kocinski in 1996, and Carl Fogarty the following year, cast big shadows over someone with my inexperience, especially on superbikes. It felt as if Ducati were having a look at me with the future in mind, but weren't too interested because their other guys were busy winning the races. It was weird, though, that I ended up in the same team – probably the biggest in the world – as Fogarty, having been born just 10 miles apart and having raced motocross at the same Vale of Rossendale club in the same shitty, muddy fields.

It was in that 1997 season that I was looking forward to come of age as a rider. But pre-season testing went badly when I hurt my ankle, then I fell off in the wet at Phillip Island and the season never got going. Things started to look up after a fourth place at Donington and then, coming into the last lap of the second race of the next round at Hockenheim, I was leading. Fogarty pushed me wide and I went into some sand before messing up, still aiming for a podium finish, by trying to dive under James Whitham. I ran wide and finished eighth. It was a real kick in the teeth but I had led the rest of the world for most of the race, and by nearly a second at one stage.

'You can ride. Don't doubt yourself too much, Neil,' I thought. Two days later I split my kneecap down the middle and tore some shoulder ligaments after getting a motocross jump badly wrong. I was back in action within a month – way too early – and twisted my twig-like leg in a fall at Laguna Seca. I did not recover from that. The momentum had gone, the demons crept in and I didn't believe the team wanted me.

Despite the disappointing end to the season I secured another factory ride with Kawasaki for the following year, with the option of another season on top. The main boost for me was that I would now be riding on Dunlop tyres, which I had liked in 500s, instead of the Michelins that I'd used for Ducati and didn't really get on with. So now I was excited again. But, having come from a successful season when Simon Crafar and Akira Yanagawa were constantly at the front and winning the odd race, the new Kawasaki bike was awful and I was not riding well as a result. The team was also running me ragged, constantly making me test in Japan, and presenting it as some kind of first-year initiation. My contract was not renewed at the end of the season.

This was my lowest point. I had stopped enjoying racing and I was seriously thinking about quitting.

'I've got a bit more money in the bank than most 25 year-olds,' I thought. 'It's not set in stone that you have to be a racer. Why should I do this for the rest of my life? If I go to England some of the tracks are a bit dodgy and if I don't do well in British Superbikes then I'm definitely finished.' I was Mr Negative.

When I went on holiday to Barbados with Kathryn, my manager Roger Burnett was working on three irons that we had in the fire, including interest from the States. However, he rang me in the Caribbean to tell me that they had all fallen through. It was on my return home when I heard that an outfit called GSE Racing was interested in me. The problem was I had heard only bad things about them. The team was owned by a self-made multi-millionaire who was called Darrell Healey. He is a bike nut with a dream to win the world championship, so it was clear they had money. But their bikes were constantly breaking down and the general impression was that they lacked some direction. Then I was told that Colin Wright, whom I knew from Kawasaki, was going to be the team manager. That changed everything because I knew that he was a good operator.

I signed for GSE Racing and went into the 1999 season thinking 'These bastards were probably laughing at me last year. This is my chance to wipe the smile off their faces.' But, having won the first race at Brands quite comfortably, I was always concerned about the championship and never threw caution to the wind. People had changed from thinking 'He's going to eat the others alive this year' to 'He's letting us down again. What is he doing?' when I wasn't winning every week. I was improving as a rider, and I certainly learned how to pass people, but I still had a lot of rough edges that needed smoothing off, and I didn't win another until the final race of the season.

GSE were a bit disappointed and made what I considered to be at the time a pretty insulting offer. We told them we would look elsewhere but then they came back with an improved deal. And I am so glad they did. The previous year I had been a little bit in the shadow of my team-mate Troy Bayliss and had to follow team orders for the final three rounds, but my attitude had changed by the following season.

It was at that stage that all the sly little digs in the newspapers and magazines were starting to get up my nose. Some of it was really personal and rude. They said that I wasn't aggressive enough and that I was riding safely because I'd lost my confidence. It just seemed to be a typical reaction from the British media. Having spotted that I was down, they wanted to stamp on me even harder. I was thinking 'Come and say that to my face and I'll break your nose.' I was livid. So, to prove them wrong, I had to dig deep and I promised Darrell that I would be the fastest in every practice session and in every race - and I believed it.

At the first pre-season test for British championship riders, we were scheduled to do two days of tests, but with an option for a third. At the end of the second day the team was ready to pack up and go home, and I had to beg them to let me do one more morning session the following day, because I knew I'd let myself down and wasn't fulfilling my promise. The old Neil Hodgson would have had a few beers and laughed 'Yeah, it wasn't a bad day. I'll do better tomorrow.' The new Neil Hodgson was asking 'Why have you not done better today?' Sure enough everything clicked the next morning and I immediately was the fastest. I knew I was changing as a rider, and I carried that aggression through into the racing, fuelled by a notorious running battle with Chris Walker. It kept me on my toes, focused and honest. Chris wanted the championship badly and was very experienced on the English circuits. He is a pitbull terrier, so I knew I had to be on the top of my game every weekend. When we started to knock each other off, it did begin to get personal, although it made for a fantastic season and brought the best out of me as a rider.

Still, that's all in the past and I won the championship, as well as managing to throw in a couple of wild card World Superbike wins at Donington and Brands Hatch. Add this to my general maturity, my growing understanding of what makes a bike go fast around a track, and I do believe that I can win the world championship this year.

I am, after all, only riding against human beings and not superstars. One of the leading contenders will be Troy Bayliss. He's my mate and a bloke whom I beat on a fair few occasions in 1999, when I wasn't riding too well. So let's bring it on! If I was riding against Mick Doohan, I might be a bit overawed. If Fogarty had still been around it would have been a lot harder because of his experience, but I would at least have been able to say to myself 'Right, this is my chance to show him.' As it all panned out, I really regret not racing against Carl as a wild card last season because I genuinely believe I would have beaten him on those days – without any problem. However, he would be very difficult to beat in a championship because he's consistently fast and he would have won it last year by 100 points if he hadn't been injured.

People might say that I'm at a disadvantage because I am with a small team and on a year-old bike. But I have been a factory rider and know that it is no better. In fact, it can be worse because you have 50,000 technicians, all speaking Italian, saying 'You need this and you need that.' I have a proven and reliable bike, I'm on the tyres that suit me the best and I have a great chief engineer in Stewart Johnstone – the best guy I have ever worked with. He walks on water and puts all the others to shame. What he doesn't know isn't worth knowing, and I have also got a great team of mechanics. The factory teams might have a bigger budget, but so what? We never cut corners on important issues.

Sure there are some big names like Colin Edwards, Bayliss and Troy Corser, and maybe even Ben Bostrom, who are all going to be difficult to beat on any given day. When news got out that GSE Racing were planning to make the step up to world level I think a few of those riders were a bit wary of the my new belligerent style, which they had seen at first hand in my two wild card rides. I don't think it particularly worried Bayliss, because that's the way he rides anyway. But Edwards made some comments at the end of season party, that I took to be aimed at me, implying that things were a bit more 'gentlemanly' on their scene.

I always used to class myself as an intelligent rider in that I perhaps use my brain a bit too much. Before, if I knew that by trying to pass a rider with a risky move might make me lose ground on the next man in front, I would bide my time until the better chance came my way. But my attitude changed last year. When I saw even half a gap, I went for it. I did it once, did it twice and by the time I had done it 25 times it was second nature. So I am not going to allow anyone to bully me out of the way, and I might surprise a few of them with the way I ride, by sticking it underneath them when they least expect it. Hopefully, sooner rather than later, I'll also fall out with someone, because that's what it's all about. It inspires me and I will be well up for it because that killer instinct is now the only way I know ...

Valencia – round 1

Monday, 26 February 2001

Maybe the pressure is starting to get to me a bit, but already I'm getting fed up with talking about myself to journalists. I suppose there are only so many questions they can ask and I know that I can only give the same answers to those questions.

'Can you fill the shoes of Carl Fogarty?'

'Yes!'

'Have you changed as a person since you were last in World Superbikes?'

'Yes!'

'Are you really capable of winning the championship?'

'Yes, for Christ's sake!'

I want people to be asking me about things that I have already done, not things that are in the future, and I'm not the kind of person to feed the newspapers with controversial lines just for the sake of it. At the start of that week, I had three trips planned to the mainland for more publicity engagements - a video about Brands Hatch, an interview for Grandstand and a feature for the *Motor Cycle News*. That meant a full three days taken out of my training schedule at the most crucial time. I knew we needed the publicity as we were still looking for a title sponsor, but it was really bugging me so I rang the GSE Racing team manager, Colin Wright.

'Colin, do I really need to do these interviews this week? I need to be as fit as I can and in the right frame of mind for Spain. What's more important – for me to stay focused on the build-up to Valencia or to be flying on and off the island all week?'

This is one of the problems of living here on the Isle of Man. It's a beautiful island and I now have some good mates there, like the World Trials champion Dougie Lampkin, with whom I train and go motocrossing. He is moving to the same apartment block as we are, which overlooks the sea on the outskirts of Douglas, but being here does add half a day onto most journeys.

'Neil, you know the racing comes first. My job is to make sure everything is right by the time the light goes to green on the grid at Valencia. Stay over there and concentrate on your training. We'll have to do the *MCN* feature because we have a great relationship with them. But I'll cancel any other media appointments from now until after the first round,' Colin said.

The Press was apparently a bit miffed and word got around that GSE Racing had imposed a media blackout, which wasn't the case as I was still doing telephone interviews from home. A media blackout would have been brilliant. Anyway, the reaction of the press wasn't my problem and I was relieved to clear the diary for a week's intense workout under the supervision of my personal instructor, Frank.

Maybe, in hindsight, that wasn't such a good idea. He had put me through my paces right up until Sunday afternoon, when we were doing a boxing workout to music as part of my final session with him. We were not hitting each other in the head, but we were also not holding back with the punches to the body – and I was getting a real hiding. An hour and a half later, on the last music track, he was just giving me one final going over. I went to throw a big 'haymaker', pivoted and went over on my ankle. I knew immediately that it was sprained. Having suffered with them before during my racing career, I knew that it could be months before it was right. This was all I needed seven days before the first race.

Even though I was in agony I managed to hobble out of the gym and drive myself home. Kathryn told me to put ice on it straight away before she went out for the evening. I was still in the chair with my leg up when she came home, because I had been unable to put enough weight on it to limp to bed. But, as it turned out, following a night out with her friends, I had to help Kathryn to bed. If the pain of the ankle didn't keep me awake, the sound of her throwing up in the toilet all night certainly did! By morning the pain was just as bad and I thought it might be broken so I rang my physiotherapist, John Barton, at 8am. His wife answered and told me to ring back in an hour. After a discussion with him, I went straight there and he told me I had saved two weeks' recovery by putting the ice on immediately. He applied a lot of electronic things like ultrasound and it worked wonders, although I'm still worried what it will be like come race day.

Wednesday, 7 March 2001

At last I'm in Valencia and it feels like the season is starting. The flight connections were not too bad as I set off from the island at lunchtime, changing for a direct flight from Heathrow. Of course, it all sounds very glamorous, jetting off to all corners of the globe, but I've already seen as much of Valencia and the surrounding area as I'm going to this weekend, and that was on the short taxi ride from the airport to the Ricardo de Tormo circuit. It is pretty well in the middle of nowhere, about a 20 minutes car ride out of the city centre.

The only other guy at the track was Malcolm Upton, who had

driven my motorhome over from England. I was really looking forward to staying in it. We had done a good sponsorship deal to buy it from a Wolverhampton company called Travelworld, whom a lot of riders use. I can never understand why some go for big flashy things worth £200,000 which lose so much value once you drive them for the first time. This is so plush and has everything you could ever want. There's a big double bed at the back, a shower and toilet, a dining area and kitchen and a sofa next to the driving area. The carpet is quite a light colour so I've already decided that it's shoes off for visitors.

There was just one problem. A bird had hit the windscreen at full pelt, cracking one side and damaging the wing mirror – and it's own wing no doubt. The window was going to cost £1,000 and the electronically operated mirror would be another few hundred.

What's more, I had paid £3,500 for a special dish so that I could watch Sky Sports. Try as I might, I couldn't get a proper reception. I probably spent another £3,000 ringing the UK helpline to try and get Simon at Travelworld to talk me through it. He was really apologetic and was almost offering to come out at his own expense to come and fix it personally. Still, it really bugged me because I was paying £32 a month and I wouldn't get the chance to use it again until Monza in the middle of May.

I had a quick look around the paddock and discovered that although we had the same equipment as the other factory teams, and were expecting enough garage space for two full teams, we had only been allocated one garage in the pits. It was going to be quite cramped in there, although, coming from the British championship where conditions were similar, I was sure we could cope. However, I knew that Darrell and Colin would not be too happy. My ankle was still pretty sore, but I managed to disguise the limp as I did not really want anyone to know that I had been injured boxing. But a great start to the season all round, eh?

Thursday, 8 March 2001

The real reason for travelling here a day early was to pose for several PR photos in our new Axo leathers but also, at the start of each season, there is always a rider briefing, where the organisers tell us of any new rules. This time, it turned into one long Troy Corser whinge. Normally, it's Pier-Francesco Chili who acts as the unofficial spokesman for the riders, but Corser seemed to be a different man this year. For a start, he had lost a lot of weight, having employed a personal fitness instructor. It was also unusual to see him without his girlfriend Sam, the rumour around the paddock was that they had split up. Most of the wives and girlfriends are quite close and like a good gossip, so this was top of the agenda when Kathryn arrived. There was a lot of sympathy for Sam as the consensus was that she had put up with a lot, and now had to go through life with a tattoo of the Corser Crocodile on her ankle!

Corser, who used to be so laid back, actually ended up arguing with Chili about one new proposal. The organisers wanted to introduce a new rule that riders who fell during Superpole, (the one-lap shoot-out to decide the grid formation), would only slip back one row of the grid. Previously, they had dropped back to 16th place for crashing on the Superpole lap. I agreed with Chili that that was harsh on the riders who had been fast all weekend but had made one mistake at the wrong time. Corser did not see it that way. He felt that if someone made a mistake early on in the Superpole lap, there would be a strong temptation to run wide and tip off into the gravel at the next corner, so dropping down just the one row. I disagreed. There was a possibility that it could happen. But surely it would not be difficult for the organizers to study a videotape of a rider, who had been perhaps one and a half seconds down on the first split, and spot them gracefully sliding wide and falling in the gravel before the second split. Surely we could just rely on the organizers' discretion.

Another thing he was bothered about was a new rule which said that we should remove our helmets after the sighting lap while we were sitting on the grid, so that we would be more recognisable to the TV audiences. My view is that we ride round a track for 25 laps with the helmet down, so what's the harm sitting for a few minutes with it off. All it does is help Grandma Jackson watching at home relate to the riders' names. Was it worth the hassle and risking a £400 fine by defying the authorities in the race? I don't think so. Then Corser argued for half an hour about plans for putting three yellow flags up when a rider falls off. The idea was to have one at the scene and one each at the two previous corners, to prevent you coming round the corner flat out. The instruction for a yellow flag was to 'Take caution and prepare to stop'. Corser argued that if you were preparing to stop there should be a red flag out.

The only thing I could be bothered having my say over was plans to stop the race if a rider needed attention from an ambulance on the track. I thought that it would still be okay to carry on racing if the ambulance was on the inside of the track, away from the race action. Of course, Corser argued against that as well, but the majority of the riders agreed with me. The decision was not to allow ambulances onto the track but if it could park just off the track on the inside of a bend, then that would be okay. So he lost out again. Colin was present at the meeting and could not believe the transformation in Corser. A laid back Australian is something he is now not considered to be! Nobody else got a chance to get a word in edgeways.

Kathryn arrived at night with my parents, after flying in from Heathrow. She would normally have travelled with me but had to attend the funeral of her grandmother that day, so she was understandably down.

Friday, 9 March 2001

Colin had planned a team meeting for the first thing in the morning.

'Now the hard work starts. Darrell has spent a lot of money to get us here and competing at world level. We all have to look the part and act the part. So keep the garage tidy. If you see a cigarette butt on the floor, pick it up. Don't just leave it there. And remember that we are all in this together and everyone in the GSE Racing team is equal, from Neil Hodgson and Jamie Toseland to the girls who prepare the food in our hospitality truck. They are slaving away all day so we'll all respect that by getting to dinner by 6.30pm. Anyone who is late will be fined,' he told the team. It was a joke but, with Colin, there's always a serious undertone. And if you step out of line, you'll be told in front of everyone. Anyway, it was quite motivating.

Colin had also decided, in view of our lack of space in the garage, to keep numbers to a minimum. That meant that our own team press officer, Kylie Maebus, was banned from that area. But, part of the deal with the MCN was that their reporter, Andy Downes, would be allowed in to give a blow by blow account of the first round. He tried to stay in the background but in such a small space, he was still in the way.

Having had a bad test here in February, my hope was that I would come here and knock a second off straight away, but it didn't work out that way. I finished the morning free practice session 12th quickest with a time of 1: 37.77, despite having

7

done a time of 1:35.8 in the December test. Even trying a softer rear tyre towards the end of the session didn't help with the grip. It's a funny old place this – the weirdest track I have ever been on. The track was a little bit greasy and the theory was that it was because the Formula One cars had tested there recently. We certainly didn't get the grip that we got in the test before Christmas.

In the afternoon qualifying session I finally did a half-decent lap on a qualifying tyre, ending the day eighth quickest with a time of 1:36.94. Corser, however, had clocked a time of 1:35.5, more than half a second quicker than Hitoyasu Isutzu, a new rider to the series on a Kawasaki. This was not where I wanted to be at this stage. I already felt as though I was on a mission to salvage the weekend.

But the first day was a bit too early in the season to start spitting out my dummy. There were an awful lot of miles to go yet. Maybe I was a little bit edgy. There seemed to be a lot more cameras trained on our garage than usual. That's fine when things are going well but it's not fine when things are bad. I wanted everyone to disappear but the media are there in the good and the bad times. Usually I can ignore it but, especially after the morning session, I was very conscious of their presence.

The main problem with the bike was the mapping, i.e. how the engine produces power by carburation. You can change it to make it softer or more aggressive on the bottom – the lower end of the revs, around 5,000–6,000 rpm – at the initial crack of the throttle. When we tested here, we had a few problems with the bike sliding around. So the guy in charge of mapping, Roberto Bonazzi, who had been seconded from Ducati, tried to make it a little bit softer on the bottom so that it didn't break traction straight away. I tried two different mappings and they felt terrible. We had gone too far from the set-up that I knew. Eventually we went back to the one we had at Donington last year and he was going to try and make it a bit more aggressive before the next day's qualifying session.

I'm the type of person who dwells on these things after the day's riding has finished. Other riders can forget all about it until the next time they sit on their bike. But, after dinner, I went back to the garage to examine the computer readings, overlays of my best lap over my second best, and to talk everything through with my chief mechanic, Stewart Johnson. We had already discussed the changes once but I wanted reassurance that he had understood what I was saying, and vice versa. It's all for peace of mind and I could study data all day, but what matters is when you go down the pit-lane and turn the throttle. If I'm going well, I don't really look at the data. But now I am probably looking for a bit of inspiration, perhaps trying to remember why I went through a corner more quickly on one particular lap than at other times.

While Kathryn went for a jog around the track, I went to borrow a video from Ben Bostrom, whose motorhome was parked next to ours in the paddock. It's the same make but different on the inside. There's an American flag draped across the wall, a guitar in the corner, a karaoke machine and it looks as though the place can be turned into a disco at the drop of a hat. From what I've heard, that's pretty well what happened when he was axed from the Ducati factory halfway through the season but he seems to be a lot more focused this year and I expected him to go well in Sunday's opening races. We ended up watching Pulp Fiction, which Kathryn did not enjoy because it did not have any romance and was too gory!

Saturday, 10 March 2001

Over breakfast, I had been thinking about the gearing. The plan was to make it shorter, so that I could get more revs in second gear at 80 per cent of the corners. However, I started wondering if it would be better to make the gearing longer, so that I could use first gear instead of second at 80 per cent of the corners. I mentioned it to Roberto before qualifying started but it was decided to stay as we were.

When Bayliss had come past me that morning, I took the chance to watch what he was doing going into the double right-hander, where I was losing time. Bayliss has got big flappy feet, so it was quite easy to see them move to change down into first gear, and that was giving him a big advantage on me coming out of that corner. Before that, people had been telling me that the Ducati riders were entering that corner in second gear, as I was, and that they were not having the same problems as me. I came into the pits and, like a school kid said: 'I knew it. Bayliss is going to first gear.'

I was also still struggling with grip and running wide at the corners, waiting to get the power on. The new theory was that it was at the front end where I was having problems with grip. However, we did not have enough time to sort it out before the end of the session since I had to make sure that I qualified in the top 16 to make Superpole. I also tried to ride smoother, because I was being told that I was too aggressive, and still my lap times did not change. At the end of the session I was 12th fastest with a time of 1:36.89.

What had really confused us is that, when we came here before Christmas and did that really good lap time on a race tyre, we thought we had the perfect set-up. Because of that, in solving the early problems with the mapping we then started to think that I was the problem and not the fact that the track had changed so much.

10

I had really wanted to start from scratch today but nothing had improved and this time, I couldn't contain myself any longer and I stormed out of the garage to the sanctuary of the motorhome. I was best out of the way before I said anything in the heat of the moment. Then Colin called a meeting at our truck.

'Has anybody got anything to say?' he asked.

'If we can, can we try and change the bike a bit?' I said. 'We need to change the bike so that it steers better for me and we also need to change the gearing.' This time they agreed.

Before the final free practice, the team altered the front offset – the distance between the centre line of the steering head to the centre line of the forks – from 27mm to 29mm so that the bike would turn in easier. We also tried a 30mm offset on the spare bike but that was a shade too much. I also settled on tyre choice with a medium hard at the front and rear. I tried a softer compound in the front but that started to walk a bit. For the first time during the weekend I felt comfortable on the bike and set the sixth quickest time of the afternoon practice session at 1:36.77. It was still not perfect but I felt that I had more control over what was going on underneath me. Ideally, I needed another two-hour session to experiment but it gave me a real boost going into the crucial Superpole lap, although I was fifth to go because the times are taken from the morning's final qualifying.

Before Superpole, I had asked the team to change the gearing slightly so that I had just a bit less revs. Unfortunately, they misunderstood and gave me a little bit less everywhere. It was a bit of a cock-up but not the only one. The team had told me to go to the end of the pit-lane to wait for my turn when the board said 30 seconds. When I got there they put the board down, so I thought there must be less than 30 seconds to go before my warm-up lap. But I ended up sitting for a minute as the temperature in the engine climbed to 116 degrees from 75. I was really pissed off because the tyres were getting colder and you struggle to get that heat back. Then, to cap it all, Chili came past for his turn, so I had to wait another 30 seconds. By this time I was shouting and swearing at the marshall.

When I eventually set off, I tried to work the tyre to get some heat into it. But on the actual timed lap, it took a few corners to get the right sort of heat and I did not ride well at the start, sliding up the yellow kerbing at turn one. My second two splits were more like what I knew I was capable of and I ended up fourth fastest for a front row start with a time of 1:36.659. That was just 0.1seconds behind Regis Laconi in second place but nearly half a second behind Corser in pole.

I was obviously a bit more relaxed that evening so a few people felt safe to pop round to say 'hello', which included my mum and dad. They come and watch whenever they can, although my dad still runs his own team – Team RCD Racing – in the 125cc British Championship with a 15-year-old called Leon Camier as their rider. But they know not to talk bikes with me. If my dad has something to say, he will say it. But they were not here to scrutinise things, just to watch some bikes and wish me well. My dad was a typical motocross parent who got all frustrated because he wanted so much for his son. Our relationship was sometimes volatile but he always had my best interests at heart and I would not have had a chance of being where I am today without his guidance and motivation. There's something inside me that says that I'd also like to be a strict dad if we have a family, but I know that probably won't be the case.

We also had another couple of visitors to the motorhome. Andrea, Jamie Witham's wife, came for a chat with Kathryn and then Carl Fogarty's wife, Michaela, popped in for a gossip after they had got back from a spot of house hunting between Valencia and Alicante. Carl was here with the Ducati team and to do some commentary for the BBC, but he found time in the morning to pop into the garage for a quick word. The cameras flocked round as it looked like he was there to give me some advice. In fact he was telling me how much he was earning now he had retired, how much he was able to eat now he wasn't racing and laughing at me because I was so nervous. Come to think of it, he did not give me one word of advice!

It has been good to read that he has me as one of the three people who can win the title this year, along with Colin Edwards and Troy Bayliss. Not everything he has said has been quite so kind down the years, but that is Carl. He will speak his mind and not worry about the consequences. If you know him as well as I, after being his team-mate in 1997, some things he says need to be taken as water off a duck's back.

Michaela was a bit worried that she was intruding by turning up at the motorhome before they served dinner in the Ducati hospitality. It made me realise that perhaps I had been a bit too much in Carl's face during that year, always hanging around his motorhome and wanting to talk bikes. There's a fine line between switching off and relaxing and keeping focused on the race.

As expected, I had a flood of calls from the Press and radio stations that night on my mobile. But again, I did not really want to be asked any more questions until I had answered a few of my own on the track, so I just left them unanswered. And, in any case, a lot of the newspapers seemed to get what they wanted by either using old quotes or taking material from our website, gseracing.com. *The Sun* did a big feature comparing my career earnings with those of Foggy. They had me down as having earned £750,000 and Carl £6million. I was surprised how close they had got with my earnings, and I guess they weren't too far out with Fogarty's. There was also a big piece on Flat Eric in *The Independent*, which he seems pleased with.

Sunday, 11 March 2001 – Race day

I'd be lying if I said I wasn't nervous. In fact I've never really felt as much pressure in the build-up to a season as I have for this. With the BBC staying with World Superbikes, and covering this race live, I felt the eyes of the nation were watching me. I also wanted to repay people like Darrell who had showed so much faith in me by agreeing to finance the move up onto the world stage. Still, I'd had a good night's sleep on the back of yesterday's Superpole and could not wait to actually get down to business.

The warm-up went well, as we had only made a slight alteration to the gearing overnight. Roberto watched me do a practice start and said I had been blipping the throttle – revving on and off. He told me to keep the revs steady at 11,000rpm and use the clutch to control the thrust forward.

At one minute to 12, my high noon had come. I took my place on the front row with a million butterflies dancing around in my stomach as the light took an age to turn green from red. Maybe I should have stuck with what I knew best after that discussion with Roberto because, when the green showed, I under-revved the engine and did not get a great start. I also had a long first gear, so it was a bit like setting off with your car in third. By the end of the first lap I was down to sixth, with Corser in my sights.

That's where I stayed for a hectic few laps. I hadn't even started to push hard, because I was still not too confident with the grip. At turn four of the first lap I turned to the left and, without any warning, the front wheel tucked and I was in the gravel. Nobody was more surprised than I was, even though I'd had a few warnings during practice at that corner. It was as if the bike was saying 'If you try and go any faster here, I'll throw you off.'

At a time when you feel that your world is falling apart, you really want to be left with your own thoughts. The BBC cameras were also in my face, which I could have done without as I was kept hanging around while I was still sweating. Then I watched the rest of the race on the monitors, trying to see how the others riders were getting on with their grip.

Back in the motorhome, I had a sulk. I don't always eat between races but, because I had not done much on the bike, I had a ham salad sandwich and a few fig rolls. I had read in a mountain biking magazine that they were a good energy food because the biscuit provides slow-burning energy and the sugary filling gives you an instant 'hit'. They also keep me very regular, which isn't always necessary after you have been sitting on the starting grid!

There was no point dwelling on the first race, though. That was history now, and I thought 'Get up off your arse and get into the garage and talk to your mechanics, because sulking isn't going to solve anything.' So, a couple of hours after the race, I went and had a chat with the guys to try and help me focus on the second race.

This time the start was much better and I moved up into third place, after surviving another real scare at turn two. Tady Okada, the new team-mate of Colin Edwards at Castrol Honda was trying to come past on the inside. There are never any gaps on the inside at a hairpin on the first lap, so I knew he was going to hit someone. You might sometimes get away with it on the outside, but not this time and he took Regis Laconi out. I didn't really see what happened and, after the first race, I would not be watching any videos to find out because I didn't really need reminding of that crash. I held onto third for two more laps, before Troy Bayliss and spaniard Gregorio Lavilla came through. Bostrom also overtook but had a stop-go penalty for jumping the start and then retired after getting another one for speeding in the pit-lane.

I was actually way too tentative in the early stages. Having crashed in the first race I did not have the confidence to push Edwards for fourth place in case I came off again and looked a complete pillock. It didn't help that the bike kept jumping out of fourth gear down the start-finish straight. That lost me time on each lap because I had to keep hitting another gear when it happened, and it did not help my concentration. Strangely, the problem seemed to correct itself with 10 laps to go. If I hadn't been taking it steady, I would at least have beaten him because I was running at the same pace as he was. So I just concentrated on holding off Yanagawa, Chili and Xaus to finish in fifth.

It could have been a lot better, but it could have been worse and I was just happy to get away from Valencia with some points under my belt. I always thought that this was going to be my worst track of the whole season and I'm fed up not to have salvaged something from both races. But only two riders, Corser and Bayliss, had a good weekend in coming first and second in both races respectively, so it was not a complete disaster.

There were things we had to work on, though. The main one was that we were down on speed. I was only 15th fastest through the speed trap at 278.6kmh compared to Corser's 287.3kmh. At national level you can make that up on the brakes but you cannot do that against these boys, and if you push any harder, you end up crashing. We also had to work on the set-up because I was going speedway into nearly every corner. I don't mind sliding a bit, but nowhere near that much. Everyone had problems with grip here but, for me, it was worse than it has ever been.

But my work for the weekend had not finished with the racing. We had not been able to find anyone to drive the motorhome back to Britain so, after spending a couple of hours clearing up and packing, we set off on a two-day drive back through France and Spain. We had been joined by a Scouser friend called Steve Brogan, who had been testing his Aprilia for the British Superstock championship at a track not too far from here. We had become friends last year while he was around the British championship paddock and he had come over on Sunday to watch the race. He talks a good race, but he's actually useless! But seriously, the lad has potential.

Joking apart, he nearly killed himself at the end of last year in a crash at the final meeting of the British championship at Donington, when he was riding a 600cc for Castrol Honda. He was practising starts and had set off, but had not been pleased with his effort and braked quite quickly to have another go down the straight. A guy called Blair Degahome was coming up behind and, having seen Steve set off the first time, did not expect him to stop and he had lost concentration. Blair hit him in the back, resulting in Steve losing his spleen, cracking vertebrae and almost losing a kidney, and the South African will never race again because of the arm injury he sustained. It was not exactly good preparation for my own championship-deciding races at that meeting!

Steve had cadged a lift with us because he was travelling on a budget. This was the first time I had driven the motorhome, so it would be good to have another male brain on hand if anything mechanical went wrong. He might even get a chance to share the driving, but we'd have to watch out for him trying to climb into bed with Kathryn and myself!

The plan was to leave at around 6.30pm and just drive for a couple of hours that night until we got to the other side of

17

Barcelona because I was fairly tired. Instead, I ended up driving for five hours and reaching France, where we spent the night in the car park of a service station.

Monday and Tuesday, 12 and 13 March 2001

By now, the rest of the team had set off on the return journey in their people carriers, which could cruise at 110mph while we could only hit 80. They were steadily catching us up and were in contact with us on the mobile phone, so the journey home became a bit of an unspoken race. Typical of that weekend, it was not going to be plain sailing. First the indicators stopped working. Then the reverse camera, which I was using instead of the wing mirror, cut out. Next the transmission went dead and I had to pull over to the side of the road. The first call I made was to the team, who were a couple of hours behind, to tell them to keep a lookout for us. As soon as I finished that call, Radio 5 Live called to do an interview about Sunday's race. It was not the best time, as I was seriously stressed.

I rang Travelworld to try and find out the problem and they said that it sounded like we had lost the power connection to the battery and described how to run it off the generator. By now, approaching Calais, my brain had stopped working. I was exhausted, depressed about the races and was tempted to drive into the sea to put myself out of my misery. I even drove into the wrong queue and had to get back onto the motorway in order to be in the correct lane. We finally managed to make the 9.30 ferry from Calais and the team arrived an hour later, so I had at least won one race that week.

I still wanted to get round the M25 as soon as possible to avoid all the traffic and eventually we stopped to rest at Oxford services on the M40. We then woke up to a £30 fine for parking

18

in the coach bay, a perfect start to another shitty day - literally. Before leaving the motorhome in Birmingham, we obviously had to empty the toilets - my job, of course. It should have just been a case of connecting the hose to a valve and directing it all down a drain, but the clip came loose and the contents of the tank went everywhere, including all over my arms. Then I had to stick my arms in to unscrew the plug. It wouldn't have been so bad if it had just been mine and Kathryn's, but I had to fish around through a load of Scouse shite as well!

All cleaned up, we hared around Birmingham for the rest of the day, as this was our last chance to buy things for the motorhome before picking it up in Monza. Finally, exhausted and nearly a week after setting off from home, we were driven to the train station with two massive suitcases each and just made it in time to Birmingham airport for the flight home. Good riddance, round one!

Kyalami – round 2

Wednesday, 28 March 2001

After returning from Spain, completely exhausted, I just wanted to hide away for a few days. There were the usual well-wishers on the phone, but no one really knows what to say and so they never end up saying the right thing. A weekend like that not only affects your riding confidence, it affects your self-confidence. I didn't even want to bump into people in the street or at the shops, whereas, if I have had a good weekend, I walk tall with my head held high and my shoulders back. I'm sure most people feel the same, whatever their job. I know that I am nowhere near as nice and chatty to people for about a week.

Once I had got my head clear, and started training again, I decided to go back home to Burnley for the weekend. We were going to be away from home for nearly two months and this would be the last chance I would get for a while to see everyone. It's the best therapy possible. These are my best friends in the world and it's not that we even stay in close contact. Lads are different to girls, who need to talk to each other every day. But, although I don't get much chance to see them, it's always as if I have never been away, and they are the only ones who know how to treat me – by not saying anything about bikes. The most anyone might say is:

'Shit weekend then?'

'Yep, shit!' And that's it. They are all probably really interested but they can sense that it's not what I want to talk about all night because I eat, drink and sleep it every other day of the week.

After three pints of Guinness on St Patrick's Day – which meant I was absolutely steaming – we went for a curry. It wasn't the best idea because, as usual, the waiters were in for all sorts of abuse. I was merry, but not as bad as everyone else and I thought 'God knows what they are going to stick in our curry. We'd better get out of here.' So we decided to leave, before they got the chance, and went to the Chinese next door. It was a good night and, after working it all off in the gym the next morning, I was starting to feel good about myself again.

Another reason for going home was the fact that I couldn't ride a motocross bike in the Isle of Man because of the foot-and-mouth disease restrictions. Trials rider Dougie Lampkin had received special dispensation from the Manx government to ride near the shore. And, if I had pushed it, they would probably have done the same for me. But, because that's not my sport and it was not essential for my training, I didn't bother as it might have caused some bad feeling. The following weekend, though, I'd have been much safer on a motocross bike.

We have put a deposit down on an apartment overlooking the sea, on the outskirts of Douglas. They are still in the very early stages of building it, but on Sunday, we decided to go and have a look at how it was coming on. We had to climb over a wall to get into the building site and there was another small wall that marked where our apartment was going to be. We were a bit disappointed because the sea views were not as good as we'd expected, but as we were looking from the ground floor, and the flat we had bought was on the first floor, I climbed onto the front wall.

'Oh, this is much better! This is the view that we'll have!' I shouted to Kathryn. 'Get up here and have a look.' Big mistake.

The wall was covered by a polythene sheet to keep the rain off the breeze blocks, so it was pretty slippery anyway. While I was helping Kathryn up onto the wall, we both lost our balance and fell eight feet below; she ended up on her backside and I landed in a handstand position on the breeze- blocks. I was in agony immediately. I had cut my hand pretty badly, my shin had been gashed straight through to the bone and I had bent back my knee.

'Shall I get an ambulance? Shall I get an ambulance?' Kathryn shouted as I laid on the floor thinking 'What the hell am I doing? I cannot believe what I have just done.' I knew nothing was broken but my knee was hurting like hell. If someone had watched us from the start they would have been thinking 'What are those idiots doing?' And that would have been without knowing that I was due to race in the World Superbike championships in South Africa seven days later. You can't wrap yourself in cotton wool, but by the same token, you don't have to go round proving you are some kind of superhero. After we had hobbled off the site it was straight back on the phone to John Barton to ask him to put my knee right this time!

Luckily, the trip to South Africa went a lot more smoothly. In fact, I have never had a better night's sleep on a plane. I'm usually terrible with names and numbers but I had kept the business card of a bloke called Josh, who works for British Airways at Heathrow and who I had met through Carl Fogarty when I was with Ducati. I had a feeling that it might prove useful one day so I gave him a ring.

'I know this is a bit cheeky because I haven't spoken to you for three or four years but, on the basis that if you don't ask you don't get, can you sort us out with an upgrade for the flight to Johannesburg?' I asked. 'If you ever need anything from me, like tickets or anything, don't hesitate to give me a ring.' And at that he came up trumps with an upgrade to Business Class. It's not that I think I'm so special that I don't want to travel in 'scumbags' class, it's just that I cannot sleep when I am sitting upright and I would never fork out for Business Class. Some teams provide this for their riders as a matter of course, though that was not my deal with either Ducati or Kawasaki in the past, so it did not seem unusual or unfair to get the upgrade.

I had about seven hours sleep on the flight to Johannesburg. The rest of the team were on a different flight because, while I was on a round-the-world ticket as we were flying on to Perth for a couple of weeks' holiday before the Australian round, they were on a standard return. I arrived about an hour before the others but Kathryn, who had travelled with the team because it was a Virgin flight and she got a big discount, had to wait for them for a lift to the hotel.

One of the team rules this year is that everyone has to wear the team travel uniform of blazer, shirt and tie. It actually looks quite smart, although I'm not sure what the rest of the World Superbike circuit thinks of us. Maybe some of them think that we think we're a bit special. That's not the case – it's just another way of showing that we are a professional outfit that means business this year. But, as I had been on a different flight, I'd been let off and I could see that some of our team, especially James, looked a bit shocked and pissed off when they saw me in jeans and T-shirt. He must have thought I had been getting special treatment. The team also looked like they hadn't had a wink of sleep between them, so I had to rub it in.

As there was nothing much to do that day, I went to the gym just around the corner from the hotel on the outskirts of Johannesburg. I went on the same rowing machine that I use at home, so I knew what I was capable of. However, we are at

5,000ft altitude here, and I felt that I had lost about 20 per cent of my performance because of that. It was a weird feeling.

James had come with us and he is a fit lad who works out quite a lot, so I challenged him to a sit-up competition with Kathryn, who has amazing stomach muscles, and myself. She can perhaps do about 500-600 repetitions in a 15-minute routine and once, only once, has she beaten me. But James didn't know this and he was really fed up when she kicked his arse. In the evening I had a massage, then it was off to our favourite restaurant, Montego Bay, in Sandton, where most of the riders seem to go and where they do the best lamb in the world. I'm never too fussy about what I eat in the build-up to races, as long as it is nothing too filling or fatty. All the restaurants seem to be in this one particular square, in a sort of massive protected shopping centre. I guess they would be too much like sitting ducks if they were out in the street on their own.

Thursday, 29 March 2001

After another brief trip to the gym for a light workout and stretches, I popped up to the track to have a look around and to prepare my rip-offs for my race visors. I always try to do this on the Thursday, when I'm completely relaxed and don't have any other distractions. This is something I have always done myself and would never entrust with anyone else. In my disorganized days, I used to do it on a Sunday morning, which is not a good idea when you are stressed out. In fact, I do not really like anyone touching my race helmet at all. Kathryn can carry it, but others might not be as careful, and the last thing you want is to discover that something has been damaged or moved just when you want to put the helmet on to go and race. It's not a superstition, just a quirk that I have.

The pre-race press conference is usually terribly dull but this one was quite lively. It's run by one of the photographers – don't ask me why – called Kel Edge. He was standing next to Colin Edwards, who didn't have a seat provided for him. So Kel asked Colin to conduct the conference and I saw a completely different side to him. He was really funny and asked us anything but questions about bikes, having a dig about things like people's golf handicaps. At one point someone told us how fast the bikes were travelling at the fast downhill left, which was about 260kmh.

'Shit, if I'd known we were going that fast, I wouldn't be here,' I said, getting up and pretending to leave. It was all good light-hearted stuff and it's great that we are not all hating each other and acting like machines.

The only person who looked to be taking it too seriously was – you guessed it – Corser. I thought it was quite revealing that, when he was the first to take his seat, he chose the one slap-bang in the middle of the row. Maybe he was playing psychological games, I don't know. But it's not something that I would have done and probably something he wouldn't have done a couple of years ago. I think I am starting to see through him.

The 20-minute drive back to the hotel was absolutely mental. The GSE team was travelling – make that racing – back in two different vans and doing just about every illegal imaginable. Bear in mind that in South Africa, and Johannesburg in particular, you have got to keep your wits about you at all times because it's not uncommon for broken down or crashed vehicles to be attacked at the side of the road. Another trend is for big bricks to be dropped from bridges in front of cars and, when they crash into them, for the occupants to be robbed. But we did not give this a second thought. The driver of our van was Troy Bemrose, the team co-ordinator, and it is very easy to egg him on.

So, when Colin was winning, all we had to do was to suggest to Troy that he should go through a red light and it was as good as done. For some reason, you seem to have a bit of a feeling that you are above the law and invincible when you are racing abroad.

Friday, 30 March 2001

After the problems we had suffered in Valencia, I half expected some work to have been done on the bike. But, between the rounds, Stewart Johnson's father had died and he had understandably been unable to put in the work that he would normally have done. It is only ever something as important as this that would prevent Stewart from working every hour available. Nothing was really said to me, but it was left that nothing major would be done to the bikes until we had got South Africa, Australia and Japan out of the way, then we could get the bikes back to Europe and make the changes before Monza.

So we started off with the setting from the winter test, when I had been quickest here by some way. Straight away, it was clear that the track was running a little bit slower. Even so, I was fifth fastest in the morning free practice session and only half a second down on the fastest time. If I had put a new tyre on for the last few laps, I would probably have been fastest. So there were no worries going into the afternoon qualifying session.

After that session, though, there was plenty to worry about.

I had asked the team to let me concentrate on a race set-up, so I did not want to use any qualifying tyres to boost my times in the afternoon.

'But if we need a qualifier, we'll stick one in,' Colin insisted.

It's very difficult to describe what was going on in my head but, whatever it was, I was horrendous and finished 16th. My quickest lap, of 1:44.353, was nearly two seconds down on Ben Bostrom, who lapped in 1:42.646. If it rains tomorrow, I will scrape into Superpole by one place. Another bitter pill to swallow was that James had finished the session around 10th, nearly half a second quicker than me with 1:42.909.

It was almost as if the adrenaline did not kick in. It was a weird feeling. Even though for most of the session I was about eighth and not doing too badly, I just wasn't enjoying it. Maybe it was because I had given myself a few scares in the first couple of laps and that had knocked my confidence. I'd probably braked only five yards too late but that means you almost run off the track. I was approaching the corner thinking 'Fucking hell, I'm going too fast', and I was trying to turn in with the front end bottoming and the tyre folding, but I still had to keep the brake on because I knew I would hit the tyre wall otherwise. When you are on top of it and riding smoothly, that can almost be a good feeling. You can smile to yourself when the back end slides and you know you have it under control. But after these moments I was almost gasping for breath because I was that tense.

It didn't help that I was trying to make improvements to the bike, yet was going a second a lap slower. You need consistency with the bike but, when we changed the gearing, we had to change it straight back. I also tried a different shock absorber, but that had to be changed almost immediately, so there was a bit of messing around, but it was still no excuse for what happened. It was almost as if a bit of complacency had crept in. Maybe I had it in the back of my mind that I knew I was good around Kyalami and didn't have to do all the usual homework. It felt similar to the disastrous winter test session that we had had at Valencia.

'I didn't want to put a qualifier in because that was your call. I just want to say how lucky we have been, though. If you had been 17th we could have been out of Superpole,' said Colin.

I was upset because I felt I had let the team and myself down. Only I really know whether I have given 100 per cent. I knew I hadn't but Colin also knew that I hadn't because he has enough experience of working with me to read my body language. So I had an hour-long 'debriefing session' with Colin. It was more than that, though. Some harsh words were said – and some that I thought were a little too strong.

'You cannot be like this, Neil. I don't think you are focused on the job in hand. Maybe your mind is on your holiday in Australia. Maybe you think that, because you are back racing at World Superbike level, that you've made it. You've got a great lifestyle, you are earning good money. Is that enough for you? Because, if it is, it's not too late for us to find someone else to do the job,' he said.

That annoyed me. I thought it was over the top. I'm only at the second race of the year and already it sounded as if my job was on the line.

'That's out of order, Colin. I'm not in any comfort zone, you know me better than that. I've had a bad session and I can't put my finger on why,' I said.

Apart from that one comment, I had found the talk with him very motivational. He's good to listen to because he doesn't just repeat everything he's said to me before. He talks about specific things and doesn't just settle for 'Pull your finger out' crap. I know that he is only trying to do the best for me by giving me a kick up the backside and it worked, but I did not feel that threatening me with the sack was either fair or effective.

When I got back to the hotel, I felt totally deflated and five foot tall. I was really upset and started to ask myself questions like 'Do you really want to be doing this? You have improved as a rider so what are doing turning in sessions like that? It's like the old Neil Hodgson again. You might as well be back riding the Kawasaki. Here you are with all this ability, a great team, and you're tossing it off in 16th place. You are at a race meeting, not a test, so there are no excuses.' So, after giving myself a really hard time and talking things through with Kathryn, I told myself, come tomorrow, I would go out and do the business.

Saturday, 31 March 2001

We decided that we weren't going to change the bike anymore, because we knew we had a setting that had worked in the winter test. And, sure enough, I was fourth in the session, as quick as anyone on race tyres, and felt brilliant. So what was all that about yesterday? I know the team were bewildered – and so was I. The afternoon session was not as good. I made a few mistakes early on and, because I knew that we had settled on race set-up and race tyres, I didn't really push too hard and finished 11th. And that earned me another bollocking.

'It's the consistency thing, Neil. You've done it this morning but not this afternoon. You've got to do it every single session. If nothing else, it helps us get some valuable data,' Colin said.

I think that sometimes, if my first couple of laps do not go to plan when I am pushing hard, the gremlins get to work. I start worrying about what's wrong with the bike and, instead of attacking every corner, I'm trying to analyse what's happening. So Colin came up with a theory that, from then on, I would have one specific thing to think about every time I went out. I might be given 12 laps to assess one particular tyre – and nothing else. It was a good idea because when I'm given a free rein to ride round without any strategy I can end up talking to myself: 'The bikes not steering as good as it was. Is it the front tyre? Is the track temperature hotter?'

When that happens, there's too much going on in my mind. I need to keep it simple.

Mind you, my Superpole lap was not much better. You basically have two choices: go out, stick your neck out and throw the thing on pole, or go out and just ride a really fast lap, without taking unnecessary risks. So that's what I did. It was nothing like my pre-season lap, which I achieved by riding aggressively into every corner. But this just wasn't one of those times when you go into the first corner and think 'Whaaaaah!' and you're on it from the word go. Instead, I had a little bit of a hesitation, which can be the difference between the front row and the second row. I still thought it would have been good enough for the front row, but it wasn't. Bostrom was quickest again in 1:41.689, while I was fifth with a time of 1:42.606. It was not bad, but I was still some way off the pace.

While my frame of mind was a lot more positive, I knew that I was going to struggle to win the race. I had seen the kinds of consistent lap times that the others had done. And I knew what I was capable of. My best bet was to get a good start and stay with them. Then, if I could improve three or four tenths a lap, I would be up there. It was possible, but it was going to be tough.

I was not the only rider having it tough. On the previous night Colin Edwards had been interviewed by a local paper and was asked by a woman reporter: 'What do you think of South Africa?'

He had replied with something like: 'It would be okay if you could nuke a couple of townships.' The quote made the front page of every local paper. Government ministers got involved because there was a general feeling that motorsport is predominantly white and that the Kyalami circuit was less friendly to the blacks than the other state-run track at Welkom, which stages the South African Grand Prix.

Colin was forced to explain himself at another press conference and told everyone that he'd been misquoted, how much he loved the country and that he often had a holiday there. He had just about won people over when he added: 'I don't know what that fucking bitch was playing at.' It was the kind of unprofessional comment that had everyone thinking 'Well, yes, I guess he is the kind of guy who's not too careful about what he says.'

Sunday, 1 April 2001

A group of lads and one girl from Halifax, who travelled around following Carl Fogarty during his career, had decided to adopt me as their new hero. They had draped flags, painted with mine and James' names, opposite the garage and were wearing T-shirts saying 'Fogarty 2000, Hodgson 2001'. From the first thing on Friday morning they had shouted themselves hoarse and drank themselves stupid. That first day had obviously taken its toll because, come Saturday morning, they were nowhere to be seen.

Then I spotted them during the pit-lane walkabout and I half wanted them to come and talk to me because it was so good to have some support, but at the same time I half dreaded it. However, t turned out that they were a really good bunch of lads and very nice people, even after I had warned them for being late!

Kathryn bumped into them later in the day and they said: 'We've been bollocked by your boyfriend for being late this morning. It won't happen again!'

Sure enough, when the team arrived at the track and lifted the garage door, they were greeted by a huge cheer and shouts of 'You're late!' They had been there since 7.30am – and were already dancing and drinking. It is people like that who make it all worthwhile.

Then, all I could hear on the line for the race were chants of 'Hodddd-gson, Hodddd-gson!' It was a great feeling and gave me a big lift, while all the other teams and riders were laughing at them.

The start of the first race did not go to plan. I didn't get a great start and the leaders were soon away from me. Then Akira Yanagawa passed me and pushed me wide, meaning that I got the line wrong into the next corner. When I went up the hill to brake, Chilli also passed me and pulled away a little bit. I already knew that I wasn't riding well.

'What the hell are you doing?' I asked myself. That seemed to do the trick and I quickly got Chilli back. On the next lap, though, I had a couple of slides in strange places. One was at the bottom of a dip and, because you are on maximum lean, it usually slides there – but not to the extent that it 'snaps'. At first I thought I had hit some oil. Then I thought it was the tyre. If it had been in practice, I would have pulled into the pits straight away. But in a race you put it out of your mind and get on with it. Two corners later I tipped the bike in and the rear end slipped a bit.

'Did it slide then, or am I imagining it?' I thought. At the end of that 10th lap the same thing happened and now I knew that something wasn't right. I looked down for telltale signs of an oil leak. There was no smoke, and I checked my boots and feet. Again I couldn't see anything unusual so I looked back to see if I was leaving a shiny black line on the track.

Chili came back past me and when I was going into the next chicane, I was praying that I was not leaking oil because, if I was, this was where the bike was going to throw me off. Nothing happened. But, as I came out of the chicane, I noticed a tiny chalkboard that could not have been bigger than one foot square with my number 100 on it.

'Shit, it is me! I am leaking oil.'

I had missed the entrance to the pit-lane so I pulled straight over to the side and parked my bike on the pit-wall, climbed over and went back to the garage. Everybody just looked at me, not knowing what to say.

'I think it's leaking oil,' I told them before a marshall turned up.

'Are you number 100? I want to see you in the Officials' office now.'

'What's this all about? Colin, come with me because I want to get it sorted straight away,' I snapped, totally pissed off. When I got there, one guy said that he could not deal with it there and then because he wanted to watch the race.

But another piped up: 'Did you not know your bike was leaking oil?' Stupid question of the season!

'What do you fucking think?' I exploded. 'The next corner is 160mph, flat out in fourth gear. Do you think I'm going to turn into there, knowing that my bike is leaking oil? I don't fucking think so.'

'Calm down, I only asked if you knew your bike was leaking oil.'

Colin grabbed me and led me out of the office and back to the garage, telling them that we would come back after the race. I was still furious and sweating when Suzi Perry from the BBC turned up and asked me for an interview. I had done one in Valencia while I was still sweating after my crash, and she had kept me waiting for five minutes, which bugged me. I was in no mood for it at that moment, so I told her I didn't want to do it.

She was not a happy girl. But it's my prerogative and I did not want to come across as being really negative answering 'Shit' to every question. It wasn't even a race they were showing live, so she could have waited. Sure, she had a job to do, but so did I. But, to her credit, she came up to me after the second race and apologised for getting the hump.

When things had died down after the race, we went back up to the office and Colin told me to try and have a better attitude. So I walked in, shook their hands and apologised for shouting my mouth off.

Claude Denin, the top man from the FIM, eventually came in and said: 'Right, Neil, your bike was leaking oil for two laps. The flag marshalls put out a black and orange flag and your number on a board on many corners. But you carried on trying to race. What's your side of the story?'

I simply told them the truth. 'The first time I saw my number – and by the way it was really small – I pulled over. What more can I say?' Then I emphasised the point that this was a dangerous track at the best of times and that I wasn't so stupid enough to ride round on a bike leaking oil.

'If I knew that my bike was leaking oil at that stage of the race, firstly, I know it's not going to finish, and secondly, it's going to hurt if I come off. And I mean hospital hurt. I am a really observant rider but on this occasion I didn't see any of the flags.'

I had to stand outside like a naughty schoolboy while the jury made their decision.

'We've looked at the evidence, we totally believe what you say because it makes sense, but we are going to make an example of you and fine you the smallest amount possible, 1,000 Swiss francs. You can appeal if you want, but that's 2,000 Swiss francs.'

We had been down that road too many times last season so I took it on the chin, but still thinking 'bastards'. I was disappointed when the team did not offer to pay the fine – about £300. After all, it was due to an oil pipe splitting on the bike. It was a really rare problem and something that nobody could have foreseen.

All this served to release some of the nervous tension I had been feeling and I was really relaxed and focused for race two. This time I didn't get a bad start and, for the first time all year, I felt as though I was right up there with the leaders. But, on two corners, my gearing set-up meant that I had really low revs. I was losing yards on the others. The new Ducatis, Aprilia and Hondas were eating me alive on acceleration with low revs so I soon started to lose touch and was running in sixth place.

At turn four, a bike came alongside me while the yellow flags were waving but I still ended up having to brake late to stop him from overtaking illegally. At the same point on the next lap, it happened again with the yellow flags still out. It was Tady Okada.

'What's his game?' I thought. But, yellow flags or no yellow flags, I knew that I could not stay with him and he had soon caught Corser in fourth place. If he had finished the race, I would have put in a protest, but he broke down later on. At one point, I was closing in on Corser in third and thought I was going to have him. I knew that nobody else was going to come past me, as I had a two-second lead on Ruben Xaus for the last couple of laps. But after Edwards had also broken down, Corser just managed to up his pace and I had to settle for fourth because I couldn't respond when he pulled two seconds on me. You can't help being disappointed when you are 18 seconds off winning the race in fourth place. Again, the bike had been 10kmh down on the fastest but Colin did point out that I had exactly the same top speed – 233.8kmh – as Bostrom who had won the race. On a good day, if I ride at my best, I can overcome those problems, but I have not done that yet and if I continue to ride like this, I'll finish fourth all year, and that's not what I'm about. So we have to improve the bike and I have to improve my riding.

I hadn't eaten much all day and so the first couple of gin and tonics in the hotel bar went straight to my head. After a really good T-bone steak at a restaurant called 'The Butcher's Shop', the team and myself headed back for a nightclub that was miles away. When we arrived I immediately thought 'This looks very dodgy!' It was all right for the others, because they did not have a girlfriend to protect and could look after themselves. I was not as drunk as they were, but I could just imagine some letching, hairy South African beefcake grabbing Kathryn's bottom and it all kicking off.

'There's something not right with this place – it looks crap,' my mechanic, Dave Parkes, agreed.

So we headed for the casino that we'd visited after winter testing. It was only then that James told us that the Honda lads had got into a big scrap at the same club a few years earlier. The whole team was out in force at the casino and it was a really good atmosphere. I played roulette all evening and won back the £300 that I had been fined earlier. Frankie, the computer technician, who is a bit of a gambler on the quiet, won £1,300 for a stake of £20, so he was fairly happy. Colin was sitting next to me and he is the world's worst gambler. He used £200 of his own money, borrowed £50 from Troy and then I leant him £50 worth of chips. But he was genuinely not bothered and blew the lot. He thought the whole idea was to get rid of his chips and could not understand that that wasn't really the point.

Monday, 2 April 2001

Having left the casino at 4am, there were some casualties the next morning, so we all relaxed round the pool in the morning. Pete Bansovic, my mechanic was probably the most bog-eyed of the bunch. After a while he stood up, complaining that his feet were hot. He took one shoe and sock off to dip his foot in the pool. Then, standing on his wet foot, he attempted to take his other shoe and sock off. It was not a successful manoeuvre because he slipped and fell into the freezing cold pool, fully clothed and carrying his mobile phone and wallet, not to mention his packet of fags. It's a wonder we didn't fall in after him we were laughing so much. He must have felt a complete tosser.

My parting shot to the group of fans from Halifax was to throw them my boots after race two but a woman was marrying one of them in Johannesburg that day and had told us where the reception was. The plan was to turn up there in our team uniform and repay them for their support by performing 'Madness' dances for them. It turned out, however, that our flights were earlier than we had thought, so we weren't able to make it and the rest of the team decided not to go.

Another rider, Marty Craggill, the most laid back Aussie you've ever met, was staying at our hotel and happened to be on the same flight to Perth as myself. We arranged to get a taxi but whilst waiting in reception we bumped into a couple of his Italian mechanics, who hardly spoke a word of English between them. However, I can understand a bit of Italian and knew that they were offering us a lift, which we accepted. Bad idea!

Straight away I knew we were going in the wrong direction so we had to turn back and probably wasted about 40 minutes. Kathryn's flight was earlier than my one and we were starting to run out of time. I was starting to get ratty, because I like everything to run smoothly.

'I wish we'd bloody got a taxi,' I whispered to Kathryn. 'They still don't have a clue where we're going.'

The next thing we knew, the passenger was turning round to us and laughing, saying in terrible broken English: 'Black man house! Black man house!'

By now I was getting really stressed. 'Airport! Get your foot down, you idiot,' I said as we drove around an industrial estate.

'Black man house! Black man house,' he continued, grinning.

Marty, what's he on about. Sort him out, will you?' I snapped, just as we went over the brow of a hill.

Then it hit me. We had driven straight into one of the townships. And the roughest township you have ever seen. As far as the eye could see there was just row after row of corrugated huts. White people just do not go there.

Kathryn had heard all the stories of tourists being mugged because they had lost their way to the airport. We had suitcases piled high in the back and might as well have had a big flashing light saying: 'Foreign tourists – please rob us!'

She told everyone to lock their doors and this time I was sweating like a virgin on her wedding night. The Italians didn't have a clue what was going on, but locked their doors all the same.

'This is going to go wrong. It's not right. You can't shout help over here. The police won't do anything. It doesn't work like that, they'll just kill us,' I was blabbering. Even Marty Craggill was beginning to look nervous. Luckily, we drove through it and found the road. The Italians had just looked on a map and tried to take the shortest route, not realising the risk.

Phillip Island – round 3

Thursday, 19 April 2001

We've been in Australia for over a couple of weeks now, but not without another minor panic in South Africa. We arrived at Johannesburg Airport to find that Kathryn's flight was over-booked by 47 people and, because she was only on stand-by, the outlook was a bit grim. The next flight that she could have got on wasn't for another two days so I thought about not catching my flight to Perth. But that would have meant I was then on stand-by, so we seemed to be going around in circles. As it turned out, they found her a space, which was a massive relief.

The time difference was only six hours so, even after a nine hour overnight flight, I didn't feel too bad. We were met at the airport by our friends from Burnley, Nick and Louise Roe, who now live in Perth where Nick works as a builder. They had found us a unit at a place called Cottesloe Beach, with a shared swimming pool and communal barbecue, and they really looked after us while we were there. So, to show our appreciation, we hosted a barbie for all their friends and family.

Perth was a really smart place and I took to it immediately. It's so clean and it doesn't seem as over-populated as a lot of cities. I'm not a city person as a rule, but this place was different. And, of course, there are the beaches. Due to a recent shark attack in the vicinity, I did not go swimming in the sea as much as I would have normally done. However, it was so easy to stay in shape and we got into a routine of jogging at 7am when it wasn't too hot and when everybody else seemed to be up and about either fishing, surfing or jogging. We also spent one day cycling around the island of Rottnest – which literally means 'rat's nest' – although we didn't see any. I was definitely getting used to this kind of active but relaxed lifestyle. They also seem to cater better for people's dietary habits. For instance, whenever I have a choice, I will use soya milk because it's healthier. If you ask for that in England, they look at you like you're from another planet. And even in Melbourne it's not that common. But in Perth they always give you the choice. So all I drank was decaffeinated cappucino with soya milk – the drink for the ultimate weirdo that I am!

However, one thing in particular in Australia is that they are so strict on speed. I got caught on a speed camera, when I was doing about 10kmh too much.

By Wednesday, when we flew to Melbourne, I was starting to get properly focused on why we were out here. The holiday was over and work was about to start again. I was in decent spirits. South Africa had ended on a kind of high note in that it had been my best race of the year. And I knew that if I could just improve slightly, while the team got more out of the bike in terms of set-up and power, we would be competitive. It annoyed me that we weren't in a position to do much to the bike until Monza, but there was nothing I could really do about it so there was no point fretting. I wanted to stay positive, especially as Phillip Island is a track that I've always enjoyed riding round, even if I've never had a good result there.

We drove down to Phillip Island, which is about 200km south of Melbourne and, if I had to compare it to somewhere in England, it is a bit like the Isle of Wight with the main town actually called Cowes. For most of the year it must be a pretty sleepy place but, in the summer, it's packed with surfers. This is now out of their main season and I'm not sure why they have this round at this time of year when autumn is approaching and the weather can be very changeable. It can be hot one minute and then a cold wind whips up from the Tasman Sea and it's suddenly freezing. There's not a lot to see on the island except a Penguin Parade, where the penguins come up onto the beach from the sea at the same time every night and since I had been here a few times racing and testing with Ducati, I had got all that tourist stuff out of my system.

We were staying at a hotel called Banfields, right on the edge of Cowes and pretty much on the road to the track. It was nothing flashy, but it meant we could be at the track in 10 minutes. And it also meant that we were well away from the promenade where they stage heavy-rock concerts right outside the main hotels for all the bikers who descend on the place for the racing.

The team were already there and I took the chance to have a big two-three hour chat with Colin at the back of the motel. We managed to go over a lot of things. He had realised that in the talks we had had so far, he had done most of the talking. So he wanted to hear what I wanted to say and how I thought things had gone up to this point. He was not trying to put any blame on me, but he wanted to know how much of the blame I was putting on myself.

One of the things I pointed out was that I'd known straight after the test in South Africa that to be fastest at that time wasn't as good a thing as everyone had made out at the time. All of a sudden, from having pretty realistic expectations, there was pressure on the team and me in particular. A fourth or fifth place in a race was now being viewed as a bad result. I also said that I was worried about the top speed of the bike although Colin argued that Neil Hodgson riding at his best would be able to make up the difference. I agreed that my riding needed to improve and we also discussed a lot of practical ways in which we thought we could improve things.

One particular thing that was niggling me was the role of Roberto Bonazzi, who had been seconded from Ducati for the season to help with the telemetry. He is the only new member of the team and might have put a spanner in the works a couple of times, because we have placed too much emphasis on his input. Don't get me wrong, he is a really good guy and I have got a lot of time for him. But it's almost as though he knows too much. He can end up bombarding us with ideas and it's got to the point that we could perhaps almost do without his input for that hour of qualifying. We are not used to his way of working. In the past it has just been Stewart and myself working really closely together. I tell him what I need from the bike and he goes off to try and provide it. It would be better if we listened to Roberto's analysis of the data after the session has finished.

Later that night I had an expert massage from a blind guy called Laurie, who I had been introduced to in 1998. It was so refreshing that everything was based on trust, which goes for the rest of the island. And, while it's is the hardest thing in the world for a lad from Burnley to do, I did pay him the full amount!

Friday, 20 April 2001

It took me a few laps to get into riding again. I had not been on the bike for a few weeks and this is a track that I've not raced at for three years. It's always harder to get to know fast tracks again, because fast corners are a shock to the system. It must be one of the most spectacular tracks, though from some angles it looks like you are riding off into the sea. The strategy at the start of the session was to put in as many laps as possible and not to tinker too much with the bike. But, just as I was starting to enjoy myself, I was called into the garage for the first time to try a softer rear race tyre and it felt better straight away. Having said that, the bike was still snaking on the brakes, especially at the hairpin corners where it was trying to back in, and it was running a bit wide on the faster turns. Stewart tried to make a change to the offset that didn't go to plan and we ended up losing the last 15 minutes. That might not sound like a lot but it can be quite important considering you only have four hours of qualifying time before the race itself. However, it's just one of those things and I finished 10th fastest but 1.989 seconds slower than Colin Edwards, who lapped in 1:34.402. Compared with the first qualifying session in the afternoon, though, that was a real result.

I started off that session again trying to get into the swing of things, testing some different tyres. Dunlop were convinced they knew what the race tyre was going to be, even before we arrived. But it had been useless in the first session, and therefore we needed to try some softer options. However, the track temperature had increased by the afternoon and the softer tyre didn't feel much better. I was starting to get a bit confused.

Then, after about 20 minutes, I was overtaken by the Spanish rider, Juan Borja. He seemed to be riding really well while I was still finding my feet. My bike was quite a bit faster than his was though, so I went straight back past him on the straight. At this stage of the weekend, I was still struggling a bit with the first corner. He had decided to come on my outside, which would have set him up to come up my inside at the next corner. I wasn't aware of where he was and I had just about hit my brake for that second corner when there was a bang. I think he must have been going far too fast to come underneath me, couldn't stop and so ended up having to use me as a brake, pushing us both off the track and onto the grass, albeit still upright.

Approaching the corner you are probably at 110mph. I was still travelling at 80mph when I hit the grass and was heading for the tyre wall. Luckily that was quite a way back and I managed to scrub off loads of speed by braking really hard. Normally the front brake will not work on grass and a crash is inevitable, but this time it gripped on the dry surface. Then I felt the front lock. It was a horrible feeling because, all this time, the tyre wall was quickly getting closer and closer although it seemed like I had ages to think about it. I realised I wasn't going to stop in time and that it could turn into a really bad crash if I hit the tyre wall. So it's an instant decision to hit the back brake, try and turn the bike and crash.

For that kind of crash you are still sitting in the riding position on the bike. So when I tumbled over, I was doing it with the bike at something like 50mph. That can be awkward as you can easily trap or twist something. Luckily it didn't happen and when I had stopped rolling I could see Borja about 50 yards away. He was also in a heap so I gestured over to him as if to say: 'What was that all about?' I reckon he realised he was in the wrong and expected me to jump up, run over and clobber him.

There was no point getting involved because my instincts were telling me to get back to the paddock as quickly as possible because, especially after what had happened in the morning, I knew that there was no time to waste. When I reached the garage, I jumped onto the spare bike. Normally, I would not be able to tell the difference between the two bikes. But this time the number two bike was not running properly – there was a slight misfire on constant throttle. And, because Phillip Island has a lot of fast corners – such as turn two where I crashed - where you do need constant throttle, it made the bike very 'surgey'. With 20 minutes remaining, it would have meant messing around with the computer and changing the mapping. So, although I went in to tell them why my times were not up to scratch, I also said that it would be better to leave it until after the session.

We took that opportunity to put on a new front tyre for me to 'scrub in' for a couple of laps. Then, as I came down the pit-lane to throw a rear qualifying tyre on for the last few minutes, the engine sounded really strange. At first I didn't know whether my earplug had become dislodged, which can make the engine sound weird. I told the team but nobody seemed to hear me and, as soon as Peter started it up, he said:

'There's something wrong with the bike. It sounds terrible.'

'I think it could be the clutch' Stewart after looking around the bike. The crash and all the messing about had left me down in 12th place at this stage, with everyone set to bang qualifiers in, which could have left me outside the top 16 and possibly out of Superpole if it rained tomorrow, which was forecast. Normally, we would not have risked me going out on a dodgy bike, but because we were under a bit of pressure, Colin told me to go out regardless.

I thought to myself 'I'm not bothered with the situation. I'm going out on a bike which could be ready to shit itself and, if I feel anything going at all, I'm going to pull in.' As I accelerated around the first corner, I felt the bike slowly surgeing, ever so slightly. As soon as that happened, I knew that it was done for. I went around turn two tentatively and then opened up the throttle. But it was really slow on me this time, so I had to put the clutch in, because I knew that I was wrecking the engine. At the end of qualifying, I was 16th fastest, 0.003 of a second faster than Stephane Chambon and more than two seconds down on Troy Bayliss's time of 1:33.577. After a nightmare session, it was a slight relief that I was at least in the top 16 and, even if it did rain tomorrow, then at least I would be in Superpole.

For me, one of the downsides to Phillip Island is that, more often than not, you'll bump into Barry Sheene. I'm not a big fan of the bloke. I first met him around 1992 and as a kid I'd been in awe of him, because he was 'the man'. Then I met him a few years later with my manager Roger Burnett, who he was very rude to. He's in a fantastic position to be an incredible ambassador for the sport in Britain, and he might have done that in his day, but now he only seems to be helping Australians. I can understand him coming to live over here because of all his injuries, but he could, I think, be more positive towards British riders including Fogarty and myself. I'm not being two faced, because he knows what I think, but I won't be going out of my way to say 'Hello'.

One guy I did want to meet up with, though, was Rod Kent, whom I had got to know when Ducati did a lot of testing at the circuit in 1996. As usual, I went to the gym every day and he was my personal trainer, a typical bronzed, happy-go-lucky Aussie, married to Carol, who worked in reception. I told them that I was sick of the Italian Ducati team always going to the Italian restaurant on the Esplanade, so they invited me round to their house for a meal. From then on, whenever I return to Phillip Island, we always meet up with them and their three sons, who are good kids. When I went there in 1998 they had split up, which was a bit strange, because I was friendly with both. They have both met other people now and we intended to go and meet Carol. Unfortunately, we ran out of time as there are only so many things I can fit into a race weekend.

For obvious reasons, I wasn't in the best of moods, but that's when it's nice to see some different faces. We went to a really nice restaurant, (although I secretly wanted to eat at Rod's house because he is a great cook), and it was good to catch up on all the gossip. We've invited Rod to the wedding, although we know that he probably won't come because of the distance.

Saturday, 21 April 2001

Today's morning qualifying session was in the worst conditions that I have ever ridden a bike. The rain wasn't a major problem, because I am quite a good rider in the wet. It wasn't completely pissing down, but the wind was unbelievable. So much so, that I was nearly blown off the bike.

The session started in drizzle though after one lap, I was considering coming back into the pits because of the wind. It whips up off the sea and especially at the part of the track suitably known as Siberia. But Colin would have gone mad if I'd done that. I thought 'If I do go into the pits, I'm learning nothing. Just ride round for five or ten laps, then go in and evaluate things.' Every time I passed the pit-lane entrance I was tempted to turn in because I was getting blown around like a crisp packet.

When I did eventually return to the garage, I had set the fifth fastest time and felt pretty good, considering. We decided to sit it out for 20 minutes, to stop the engines from being needlessly worn out by riding round in the wet and to see how fast everyone else was going. But, during that break, the rain came on really strongly.

We then tried a new wet weather tyre but, because it was new, I nearly high-sided at the Honda Hairpin on my first lap back out. At Siberia, it spun completely, so I did not even complete a fast lap on it. I came straight back into the pits and said:

'What's this tyre? It's completely shit. Stick that first one that we tried back in.'

I went faster, felt very safe and finished the session sixth fastest and was confident we had found the right tyre for wet conditions. I thought 'If I stick my neck out tomorrow, I'll probably go three or four seconds a lap faster and even start to slide it.'

For the afternoon free practice, or Superpole warm-up as I call it, the rain had stopped so we tried a softer race tyre again. But I was continuing to struggle and my times were nothing special. It was still sliding everywhere, which I couldn't believe. It had gone past its best after about three laps and I was literally speedwaying into some corners. Half way through the session we put a harder race tyre in and my times improved no end. Then, right at the end of the session, I stuck a qualifier in, just to get used to it before my Superpole lap. For the first time all weekend I felt comfortable on the track and I ended the session fourth fastest, about three quarters of a second down on Corser's time of 1:34.767.

The Superpole was declared 'wet', which means that riders have 40 minutes in which to complete 12 laps and their best lap time counts. If they do more than 12 laps, their best time is deducted for every lap over the 12. Although it was declared wet, the track was actually mostly dry, apart from a couple of slightly damp sections, especially at the Hayshed. That's where Troy Bayliss crashed on the first lap of Superpole, planing the skin off two of his toes because he wasn't wearing titanium toe-sliders in his boots. If it had been the normal dry Superpole, I would have been the first one to go and would have had the worst of the drying conditions. This way, though, everyone was on a level playing field.

We had two qualifying tyres at our disposal, a soft one and a really soft one. Everyone else went out on the softest one straight away but Colin said it would be a good idea to use the less soft one for a couple of laps, just to get dialled in again. As it turned out, most riders wasted their best tyre because the red flags came out when Bayliss crashed. When I switched to the softest tyre I was immediately up on my best time until I came across Broc Parkes, who was on an out-lap but was on the race line and cruising.

That messed me up but it wasn't his fault, as there were no blue flags out to warn him. I came in again, put a new soft tyre on and knocked almost a second off my best time but then, on my final qualifier, I lost concentration on the second corner of my flying lap. 'Don't high-side round here because it's a bit damp on this line,' I thought, and so I didn't turn the throttle at the right moment. If that had not happened, I would probably have ended up on pole, because I had the middle section spot on.

When I came into the garage after my 12 laps I was quickest with a time of 1:33.740, although a few other riders were still on the track. The team greeted me as if I had won the race. I suppose it was a breakthrough and Darrell had a real look of relief. But I was not all that fussed and thought 'You shouldn't act so surprised. This is where I am meant to be.' Considering we'd had a bit of shit to put up with, it did no harm to see some smiles again. It turned out that Corser went quicker with a time of 1:33.576 and I guess I had to be pleased with second, particularly in those windy conditions.

During the evening meal with the team, which was at the same restaurant that we had been to with Rod the previous night, I felt very relaxed and confident. I have been on pole before and known that it had been a bit of a fluke. But this time I knew that I had a good set-up for the dry and the wet, and that I was enjoying riding round in both conditions. I'm ready for anything tomorrow brings.

Sunday, 22 April 2001

When I pulled back the curtain this morning, it was absolutely lashing down – and obviously had been for some time. It's a horrible feeling and it doesn't help when you open your motel door and it's nearly blown off its hinges by the wind. It was the most miserable, cold, grey day that you could imagine. And, while I hadn't been worried about a wet race, these conditions were far from ideal!

The only thing I do differently as far as preparation goes is to tape up the top of my visor to make sure no water gets in. I am pretty sure I don't need to because my Suomy helmet is really good for keeping it out. I know Suomy probably don't like to see me doing that, as it's hardly a good advert for a helmet which is for use on the roads in all conditions, but the taping has become part of my routine now. However, let's argue about that one at a later date because, once the water is in, it's too late!

During the morning 20-minute warm-up session it became clear just how much water was on the track, but at least my oversuit was keeping the wind out and I didn't feel too cold. In fact, because I was only out there for six laps, and even though the rain was already bouncing off the track, I felt quite snug because the water had not had a chance to seep through. The session was a disaster, though. The front of the bike felt fine but I was having a lot of slides at the rear, bearing in mind that 24 hours earlier that had not been the case. That was the only clue we had that the tyre was not going to be able to cope with the amount of surface water.

I had convinced myself that I needed to stay out for as long as possible, because the weather looked set for the race but suddenly, I was being blue flagged. Somebody was catching me up fast, so I pulled over to see who it was. It was Edwards and I tucked straight in behind him to try and have a look at what he was doing differently. When he went into turn three, a fast left-hand kink, as though it was dry, I shut my throttle off because I was sure that he'd be going down. Instead he pulled 30 yards on me without any effort. I tried to stay with him around the next two or three corners until I had the biggest two-wheel slide possible at the fast Hayshed section. Again, Edwards didn't have a problem and had cleared off by three or four seconds.

At the end of the warm-up I looked at the times and I was the fastest rider on Dunlops - but in about tenth place. Edwards was quicker by about four or five seconds.

'What's the catch here?' I asked Higgy, our Dunlop technician who worked with us all last year so he knows his stuff.

'We're struggling,' he replied. And when he says that, you know you are in trouble. 'But the majority of Dunlop riders are sticking with the tyre that you've just been out on,' he added.

It wasn't obvious that I was making a big mistake and sometimes it's better sticking with the devil you know. Having said that, someone might as well have opened up a tap to drain out all my enthusiasm. I knew I was in for a really difficult and long race. I might as well have got my coat and set off for Japan there and then, but my realistic aim was to get a good start and be in the top five or six by the end of the first lap. I knew I was going to be passed by Michelin riders and not be able to do a thing about it, but by the same token, I knew that I might still end up on the podium if I managed to stay upright.

'Look, the pair of you, just remember that everyone crashes at this track when it's wet,' Colin said at the pre-race team talk. Jamie Whitham also came up to me and told me to make sure that I finished the race.

'I just want to say, Colin, that if I do fall off, I haven't meant to. I've listened to this conversation, and I am going to use my head but anything could happen in these conditions,' I warned, knowing that I was on a bit of a hiding to nothing. Had I lost the front end on the first lap, I knew that Colin would be like 'I told you so'.

I'm usually a really good starter in the wet because all I think is 'supermarket traffic lights' – I've been to the supermarket and got all my food on the bike so, when the light turns to green, I mustn't break the eggs. It's the same for a race. When the lights go out, let the clutch out and almost stall the bike and you can guarantee that you will be in the top three going into the first corner.

I entered the first corner in 22nd place from second on the grid. And that's some going. It was, without doubt, the worst start I have ever made. I'd done everything by the textbook, such as parking the bike outside the white markings, so that the first thing the tyre found would not be the slippery white paint. For the warm-up lap I'd let the clutch out slowly then accelerated hard and couldn't believe how much grip there was. Thinking that everyone else would be too tentative, I decided to give it that little bit extra for the actual race start.

But this time, as soon as I let the clutch out, the back wheel spun instantly and I hardly moved an inch. It felt like I was going backwards so I started to panic. Two things went through my mind - the devastation of the fact that I wasn't moving and the realisation that, with all the spray flying around, I was going to be collected from behind. So I short-shifted into second to try and get some more traction, but by then it was too late. I wasn't actually last into the first corner, but I felt like it.

I knew that there was no point going into the first couple of corners trying to take on the world and pass everybody because that way I was going to crash, for sure. So I ended up not passing anyone and that was difficult to hold back, knowing that there were some Aussie privateers ahead of me. After four corners, when I could pick things out a bit better, I saw James ahead of me. That made me laugh because Colin had said that it would be easier for him starting in 19th because he would be able to judge things better.

'Easier for James? By the time he gets to the first corner there will be so much spray around that he won't know which way the track goes,' I'd replied. And I wasn't trying to pull his leg or piss him off, it was just a statement of fact.

'Thanks for your encouragement,' James had grunted.

I eventually started to pick people off, including James, and I couldn't believe how slow everyone was going. In that group were people like Bostrom and Chili and I knew that I was going to have them for breakfast. A few corners later someone tried to out-brake Craggill, sent him wide and, as he was coming back inside, I decided to take him at the hairpin by putting my bike in his way. It was not the nicest move I have ever made, but there was nothing illegal about it. Either his reactions were too slow, or he did it on purpose but, when I went underneath him, he turned straight into the back of my footrest instead of just lifting his own bike up and allowing me through. He stayed on, but he pushed me down and it doesn't take much contact in those conditions, especially when you are on the limit of adhesion.

Your brain doesn't have time to think 'Oh shit, I'm going to get run over.' All I was thinking was 'I'm down. I can't believe it, I'm down.' I had no idea, until I watched the video after the race, that Craggill was inches away from hitting me as I was sliding along and he came through.

When I came to a halt in the mud, I could see that the back wheel was still spinning. I sprinted over to it and grabbed the clutch and throttle because I knew that if the bike were to stall, my race was over. But these bikes are really hard to pick up by the handlebars so I had to wait for a marshall to arrive, while keeping the engine running. When we did manage to pick it up I immediately saw that the front brake lever was at a vertical angle to the handlebar. That's because, halfway along, there's a nut and bolt that allows the bar to bend rather than snapping. All you have to do is bang it back into place. This is the first year that I've had one and I couldn't believe how well it worked. It saved my race because, although half my footrest was missing and my back brake had snapped off, I could get by with those problems because I don't use the back brake anyway.

When I rejoined the race, in last place, the first lap was really slow because I had to test the front brake a couple of times and it had a bit of dirt in it. The lever was really sensitive and a long way out and it probably took four laps before the grit worked its way out and the brake bedded itself back into place with a good feel.

The only plan then was to just ride round and it wasn't long before I got the blue flag after being lapped by Edwards. I wasn't going slowly, but there was nothing I could do about it. Then, the only consolation for me was to pass James after he had run on at one point. I finished 11th out of 15 finishers and, ironically, 10 seconds behind Craggill – and I'd spent a minute on the floor! So the best I could have done was probably fifth.

'You came underneath me and gassed it too early. You went one way sideways, then the other, and I hit the side of your bike,' said Craggill, when I bumped into him at the circuit café after the race. That's not how I remember it and you normally remember it if you have a slide like that.

In hindsight, it would have been better for us to have used the 20 minutes of Saturday qualifying that I sat out during the rain. That would have given us the chance to test the other Dunlop rear tyre, the one that I only tried for one lap – but in the lighter rain. It was the same soft rubber compound, but it proved to have the best pattern cut into the rubber for today's flooded conditions. It's all about how the pattern disperses the water from the track. It's quite annoying that the best tyre slipped through the net. If the weather conditions had been the same today as they had been yesterday morning, the riders on Dunlop tyres would have been at an advantage. In those flooded conditions the very soft rubber of the Michelin wet tyre generated much more heat so, for their riders, the tread pattern was irrelevant.

Our Dunlop man put his hand on my rear tyre straight after the race and it was stone cold. Normally his hand would stick to them. That's why we were aqua-planing around the track and that's why we were two to three seconds a lap slower. Normally, half a second is a big advantage. But that kind of difference means that you're in a completely different race.

I don't want to put the old record on, the one which plays 'Why me? What have I done to deserve this?' That's the old record from Neil Hodgson's world superbike career of years gone by. Last year, I could do no wrong. So far, this year, it does appear to be exactly the opposite. There had been a light at the end of the tunnel after Superpole here, but it had been switched off just as quickly with that fall. If nothing else, I am a realist and I can't help but think that I'm not going to be world champion. (The consistent way that Troy Bayliss is riding, my money is on him at this stage.) And, normally the best remedy is to put the record straight in race two, but in some amazing scenes that were to come, I was even denied that chance.

During the break between races the rain had not stopped for a second and, for brief periods, was coming down even heavier. The Supersport race went ahead but their conditions were barely fit for racing and when I ran from our cabin into the garage to get changed for race two, there was another massive cloudburst. Then I noticed that there was a river running down the side of the garage, where the mechanics stand, and I knew that it had not been there for race one.

'Bloody hell, Neil, it's really coming down hard now. I don't know if they are going to run this,' Colin said to me 15 minutes before the scheduled start.

'No, they will do,' I said trying to blank the possibility out of my mind because I wanted to prepare myself mentally in the normal way.

'Even if they do start the race, I'm not sure I'm going to let you out in it anyway,' Colin said.

I was bursting for the loo, but that would have meant running out into the rain again to go to the toilets. So finding an empty bottle, I filled it at the back of the garage. Darrell put his hand on my shoulder, at first not realising what I was doing, and said:

'You're a dirty bugger. That's the second time today I've caught you doing that. I was actually coming to tell you that, if you're bothered about what I've been thinking, I don't want you to go out. It's up to you, but these conditions are atrocious.'

It was really nice to have that reassurance. Here's a guy whose hobby is costing him millions, he's come half way round the world to see me do well but he still has his priorities right. His words took all the pressure off me. If anything, it made me want to race for him all the more.

Then Corser walked past the front of the garage holding an umbrella. He stopped, peered in and asked me:

'Are you going to go out in this?'

'Nope,' was my instinctive reaction, because the monitors were now showing different sections of the track where corners were properly flooded.

Kathryn was pacing up and down, chirping: 'You can't go out in this. Nobody in their right mind can race in this, it's got to be cancelled.'

Gradually, it must have been sinking in that there was a good chance it was not going to go ahead, because I could feel myself relaxing and starting to joke about things. Then, the monitors showed pictures of Corser arguing furiously with Davide Tardozzi, the Ducati factory team boss. I had a chuckle about that as well until, suddenly, I thought 'Neil, what are you doing? For all you know you are going to be out there racing in this in a few minutes. All that's going to happen is its going to be put back 30 minutes or until it stops raining. Get focused.' So I walked away from the screen and had a stretch in a quiet corner.

Deep down, though, I was now seriously hoping that it was going to be cancelled. The track was flooded and I was on tyres that were three or four seconds down on other riders. But, at the same time, I didn't think for a second that it would be cancelled because it would have been the first time in history that it had happened.

When the news did come through that it was off, it was like somebody had popped my balloon. I was totally deflated and empty. I should have been jumping for joy and relieved. Perhaps it's because, after building yourself up so much for a race, it's hard to replace that feeling of anticipation.

For the first time in the season, though, I'd been really impressed by Corser, but he should not have been forced into making that stand. The organizers should have announced a 30-minute delay, five minutes before the pit-lane was opened. That would have calmed everything down. And, if conditions had not improved by then, they could have delayed it by another 30 minutes. Then, if there were still no change, it would have had to have been called off. It was so logical it was frightening. Sure, they have to take television schedules into account, but to sit everyone on the grid, getting soaked to the skin, before making a decision didn't make any sense whatsoever. If they had got us onto the grid, they would probably have started the race. The bottom line is that a rider's safety has to come first, and it should not have been down to Corser to make that point, so there shouldn't be any repercussions.

It would not have been possible for me to make that kind of stance. Corser effectively runs the Aprilia team. It seems that whatever he says goes. In our GSE team I am a rider, nothing more, nothing less. And I'm paid to ride, not make policy decisions. But I do think the riders should have more of say in things that affect them. It can only help if we can speak with one voice and if we take democratic votes on certain issues. At the moment Flammini have too much control and can easily shift the goalposts. Riders have contracts with their teams and if, for argument's sake, the organizers decided to do away with prize money next year, there would be nothing you could do about it if your team agreed. At the end of the day we have all got mortgages to pay and you don't want to rock the boat as individuals, so it can only help to have a rider representative, especially when it comes to safety matters. And it would have avoided all those scenes in this instance.

I was asked by a few newspapers for some quotes about Tardozzi's actions. On the face of it, it had looked like he was trying to get the race to go ahead when he was arguing with Corser. It wasn't until later that night that I discovered he was just telling Corser that he was going about it the wrong way and that one rider did not have the authority to try and persuade other riders not to go out on a sighting lap. There was nothing I could do about the quotes being published, but I did clear it up with Davide.

Having said all that, and though I'll give both the benefit of any doubt, I can't help but feel that both Corser and Tardozzi had the championship in the back of their minds. Corser was on Dunlops and knew that he was not going to pick up many points.

Tardozzi knew that Bayliss was, at worst, going to pick up another 16 points for third place as long as he stayed on his bike.

At night, after a jacuzzi in the room to wind down, we met James and Andrea Whitham in the hotel bar for a couple of gin and tonics. They say that gin can make you depressed and I did become a bit moody. But the entertainment came from Carlos, the top guy at Motorex, who sponsor our team. He's a really cheeky Swiss guy who has the thickest skin in the world, and always comes back for more, no matter how much you offend him. Anyway it turned out that he had won a bet with the chef at the hotel with the result that he was cooking the pasta starter tonight.

From a bit moody I'd become really argumentative at dinner and I even snapped at Darrell, who was sitting opposite me, and that's really unusual. I think he thought I was joking, so I got away with it and thought to myself 'Whoa! Pull back driver.'

Yesterday, Colin had introduced me to a guy from Budweiser who, on first impressions, appeared a bit scruffy. As we were still looking for a title sponsor, this was the kind of guy we were happy to have around and he was allowed to hang around the garage all weekend with his friend. I thought nothing more of him until Darrell got up to go to the toilet and this guy, I think he was called Chris, tried to sit where Darrell had been.

'I'm sorry, Darrell's sitting there,' I said.

'Oooooooohh! Sorrreeee!' he said sarcastically, before finding another place. Then, for the rest of the evening, he did an awful lot of taking about himself. He collared everyone for about 15 minutes and, as a result, we tended to split up rather than sticking together as a team as we normally do after a race.

'How would you like Budweiser on the side of your bike?' he asked me. What exactly did he want me to say? That I'd hate it?

'What do you think you could for Budweiser? Do you think you can win the world championship?' he then asked. I'd been working hard all weekend and the last thing I wanted was to be interviewed by some complete stranger.

'I'd try to do whatever you wanted me to do?' I replied, curtly.

It turned out that he went through the same questions with the rest of the team. But, having said all that, he paid for the dinner, which came to £1,000, so it will be interesting to see what develops.

Monday, 23 April 2001

Stewart was sharing a room with Colin. At a quarter to six the following morning he came back to the room, got four bottles of Budweiser from the mini-bar and walked down to the Esplanade to drink them with Ashley to watch the sunrise. That would have been a good idea, except that it was still pissing down!

An hour after they went to bed, I was up preparing for a shopping expedition with Troy Bemrose, the team co-ordinator. He's the nicest guy you could ever want to meet and does a lot to help me out. But he has got no idea about style. So, when he said that he was off to buy some clothes, I insisted that I went along to act as his fashion guru. It was an unsuccessful shopping trip that probably lasted two hours – and that's pretty difficult on Phillip Island. I've also put him on a healthy eating regime, because he is a bit overweight and knows nothing about dietary habits. I've set him the target of losing a couple of stones.

It was time to drive back to Melbourne but, because our connecting flight to Sydney was delayed, we almost missed the flight to Tokyo. Kathryn was already in Sydney waiting for me, because her stand-by ticket was with Ansett and not Qantas. Travelling separately can be a bit of hassle but it saves more than £1,000 so we both think that it's worth it, but she had been getting quite anxious because she thought she was going to have to travel to Japan on her own.

Sugo – round 4

Thursday, 26 April 2001

After all the panicking about flights in Australia, we decided on our way over to Japan that it would work out better if Kathryn missed this round. The way her work schedule had been panning out, if she stayed in Japan she would not have been able to go to Monza for the next round. She would also have had to leave on the Sunday night, which was always going to be a load of hassle. Then she would have been away working for the week that I would be at home before travelling out to Italy. I was planning to stay in the motorhome at Monza, so it would be better to have her there. At least in Japan I'd be with the rest of the team in our hotel, so it wouldn't feel as if I was completely on my own.

'It's got to be your decision,' I said. 'I know you've never been to Japan but, if you want my honest opinion, it would be better if you went home now and then came out to Italy.'

It had been a terrible flight from Sydney. I had stayed awake to watch one of the films but, with four minutes remaining, the screen went off so I missed the bloke being rescued/killed by the terrorists. Then I couldn't sleep because I was so annoyed and was wondering what had happened to the guy who had been kidnapped. When we landed at Tokyo, Kathryn stayed on at the airport to catch the next flight to England, which was quite an emotional moment.

Some people think that it's down to me being tight that she is still working at all. That's just not the case. She likes to feel that she has her freedom and her own money, so that she's not relying on my income 100 per cent. Secondly, because we live on the island, it allows us to have cheap flights on and off. But I have told her, especially as we are getting married this year, that she can knock it on the head straight away the day that she no longer wants to work.

We've been together for four years now and, especially over the last couple of years in the British championship, she has been a brilliant help organizing passes for friends and family. Everybody knows that if they want to get in touch with me at a race meeting they have to call Kathryn's mobile. Mine is switched on but I don't answer it because I don't want to be hassled. Even if she does try and involve me or ask for help, I still try not to interfere. I'm understandably edgy and it's one worry that I can do without. We don't have those problems in Japan, though, so that was another reason why, of the two, this round was better to miss.

Some riders can't be without their wife or girlfriend at a meeting but I wouldn't say that I fall into that category. For the last two rounds in South Africa and Australia, it's only really when I've shut the hotel room door that it's been great to have her there. It's great not to be on your own, and especially when things aren't going well. Roger Burnett, my manager, is over here commentating for the BBC, so he can be my Kathryn when it comes to having a whinge this weekend.

And was I ready for a whinge by the time we reached Sendai. Carrying luggage from a five-week holiday, we had to get a train from Narita Airport into Tokyo, which is about 60 miles away. I'd not had a wink of sleep on the flight and it was a real relief to get off the plane and loosen my tie, because the shirt is made of a really itchy material and it was beginning to annoy me. Then we were straight onto the bullet train from Tokyo to Sendai, a provincial town in the north that is about the size of Manchester. Luckily, because I was with the team, I didn't have to use my brain to find my way around as I could just follow them like a sheep. Japan is not the easiest place in the world to find your way around.

The JR train system runs like clockwork and you only have a minute or so to board and find your seat. But that was a real problem for us because Frankie, the computer technician, had injured his knee playing basketball in the hotel grounds on Monday morning – whatever he touches seems to turn to disaster. He could hardly walk and was a real liability, so it was a real relief when we reached the hotel at lunchtime and I could dive into the shower.

Where did we go to eat on our first night in Japan? A curry house of course. I had actually been there before and knew that it was pretty good. We'd decided that, if we were going to go there, it would be better sooner rather than later in case any of us ate anything dodgy. But it was a good meal and they did the best Indian bread in the world – bar naan!

On Wednesday morning, James and I went to a gym around the corner from the hotel. At the entrance was a mat where we had to take our trainers off and put on some 'girlie' slippers – which I think James rather enjoyed. We weren't allowed to wear outdoor trainers, and so they tried to hire us some for about £16. We told them that they didn't have our sizes, and instead we cleaned our own trainers with a rag.

Then it was up to the track, for a walk round the circuit with James, who had never been there before and wanted some advice on the lines and the gearing. It's a fairly spectacular place, set in a massive sports complex in the hills about 30 minutes drive out of Sendai. There is a huge mountain range in the distance, which is a big skiing area in the winter. And, while it was nice and sunny, it was not stiflingly hot as we were quite high up.

I then did another lap with Stewart, because it's important to remember that it was also his first time round here. He is a mine of information and was brilliant at analysing the nature of the track and coming up with ideas for us to try. It's one of the best things we have ever done and we'll be doing it at every meeting from now on. He's usually quite quiet and doesn't open up too easily unless he has had a beer when he doesn't make too much sense, so it was also nice to have a good chat.

The team was in pretty relaxed mood and chatted in the hotel bar after a disaster of a meal at one of their restaurants. All the orders were messed up, which worked out fine for me as they brought me salads. The Japanese try really hard to please but the language barrier can be a real problem and it probably doesn't help when we try to confuse them all the time with cheap laughs!

As we were at a bit of a loose end on Thursday, we went back up to the track, where I prepared my visors before returning to the hotel in the afternoon. I had become rather an expert on the 10-pin bowling game in the hotel foyer. I was playing this when I heard some girls talking about me from behind one of the pillars. They were part of a BBC documentary team, making a series on biking events around the world. The programmes were to be presented by Mary Anne Hobbs, the Radio One DJ, for the launch of the BBC3 channel. She had interviewed me in the break between races at Brands Hatch the previous year and had seemed very enthusiastic – and I would never knock anyone for their enthusiasm. I went over to say hello and her team arranged to do some filming over the weekend.

That night, James, Darrell and myself decided to be a bit more adventurous with the food and visited a Japanese kobe beef restaurant. Kobe beef is an expensive delicacy over here, made from cows that have been fed a diet of beer and massaged throughout their lives. But this place was a disaster. There were only two waiters on duty, so it took ages to be served. And, when the guy did bring it out, he was sweating profusely and the sweat was dripping onto the food. It didn't do a lot for my appetite. James and Darrell had ordered tongue and were literally nearly sick when they tasted it. But I suppose you have got to accept these things when you are in a place like this – and it's not as though I'm a really big fan of the country. They do things differently to us and sometimes it's better to stick with things that you are familiar with, especially where food is concerned.

Friday, 27 April 2001

The one drawback about Sugo is the distance to the track from the centre of Sendai, the only place where you can really stay. The traffic is pretty heavy but we decided not to go up with the team, as they were going on the shuttle buses organised by the hotel which were a bit too early for our needs. We had hired a van, so Troy drove Darrell, James and myself to the track at around 9.30am, in plenty of time for the first qualifying session at 10.45am.

I tend to leave breakfast until the last minute but James had been up for a while and was waiting in the hotel lobby for everyone else to arrive. In one corner was a grand piano, so he asked the manager if he could have a play. I think the bloke was a bit worried that he was going to hear something awful, but James is actually very good and, before long, all the little Japanese girls who worked in the hotel had gathered round to listen to him tickling the ivories.

'Ahh, so! Mister James, you so tawented!'

It was a bit of a struggle from the word go, and you can't make excuses about it being a strange country etc. Once you are on the track, it could be anywhere in the world. The only thing that is very different about racing in Japan is the number of very quick local wild cards that enter for this round. One guy, Makoto Tamada, was fastest from the very start of the session. And, when I looked at the times, he was more than two and a half seconds faster than I was – 14th quickest with a time of 1:31.989.

'Where the hell am I going to find two seconds a lap?' I thought. I'd been riding hard in that session, so I was already starting to panic. Earlier in the morning I had asked Stewart what the score was regarding tyres over here.

'There are three compounds in the medium English 747s, there's a 587 to try and then there's a Japanese compound, which was the race tyre here last year. It's quite a soft rubber, though, so if the track temperature is low, we won't be able to use it. The temperature needs to be around 30C for it to be effective,' he told me.

In the first qualifying session, I'd reduced the gap to Tamada to a second and a half. His best time was 1:28.658 while I was now ninth fastest with 1:30.164 but with only three championship regulars – Corser, Edwards and Lavilla – ahead of me. By now it already looked like being a Dunlop weekend, as Bayliss was way down in 15th place and really struggling. I would probably have gone even better if it hadn't been for a clutch problem on one of my bikes. Everything could feel normal but, when I braked at the 100 yard board on the straight and grabbed the clutch to go down the gears, there would be no tension. Blipping the throttle while kicking the gear lever tended to upset the bike although some riders, like Ben Bostrom, do it that way normally.

In the end, it was a bit of a disjointed session. We'd had a plan to change the gearing to give me less revs all around the track. Stewart also had a plan to improve things by changing the rear shock. He's been working his bollocks off this weekend. Maybe, up to this point in the season, he has not been as accurate as he was last year, but I think that has been down to the information I've been providing for him. If you're not on the limit, your information can be inconsistent. That hasn't been the case this weekend. From the first thing this morning I felt on it, even though it took me a bit of time to get dialled into the track again. However, every bit of information that I've given to Stewart has led to a noticeable improvement so far.

The first time the clutch went was after six or seven laps. Then, after I'd come in once, it went again on the first lap back out, by which time I was starting to get a bit stressed. Colin told me to go out on the old bike, which would normally have been fine but it had the old gearing and old shock set-up. To make up for it, though, we used the Japanese tyre for the first time. The bike felt terrible but straight away I knocked three-quarters of a second off my time. It was a great feeling and I knew that, with the proper set-up, I'd be able to go even faster.

The Japanese Dunlop tyres are totally different to the English equivalents. The English ones have decent side grip and really good drive grip, so you are skating when you are actually in the corner but can shoot out when you pick the bike up. The Japanese ones are the opposite – they have unbelievable side grip but no drive grip. And, after the first five laps of the afternoon, I'd already complained that I didn't have enough side grip in the turns. Whenever I was touching the throttle I was losing control and the bike felt like it wanted to 'high-side.'

This tyre was the perfect solution for those problems. It enables you turn the throttle so early that it's almost scary as the tyre is designed for a typical Sugo second gear corner, where you get in and then immediately get hard on the throttle. But, although you start to slide when you pick the bike up, you can rest assured that you're not going to 'high-side' at this point of the corner. I did about 15 laps on this tyre, because the traction breaking took some time getting used. After the session we also decided that Stewart would make some more changes to the rear shock to give me even more rear grip by tomorrow.

It was fairly impossible to miss Mary Anne and her television crew throughout the day. For a start, she was wearing an unbelievably bright set of yellow leathers. Then, when they were not filming she went to stand on the pit-wall. And, whenever James or I rode past, she jumped up and down, shouting and clapping her hands. It was quite a spectacle and Colin thought that it was putting Skip and Pete off from doing the boards, so he asked her as politely as Colin can, if she'd mind not standing there during the session.

We'd agreed to do a 20-minute interview at the end of the day, which was a bit inconvenient because we wanted to get back to the hotel. But, in this business, exposure is everything – for myself as well as the team. Even if we got a five minute slot during a pretty big series, it would be worth it. I remember doing a big interview for Eurosport last year, unsure of what I would get out of it, but it was a brilliant one-hour programme and great for my profile. You have to take the good with the bad and we went out of way to make ourselves available for the interview, which eventually lasted for an hour and 10 minutes, so I did well not to be immature and spit my dummy out.

With the interview going on for so long it meant that we were starving, so Troy dropped James and I off at an Italian restaurant in the city centre. This trip has meant we've spent a lot more time in each other's company and we've started to gel very well.

During testing at Valencia we were total strangers with just a mutual respect for a fellow rider, and it took until the test in South Africa for us to start to get to know each other and have a bit of banter. When the season started, and James went quicker than me in the first session in Valencia, I was really pissed off, and he seemed to become slightly cocky. I can't blame him, because I'd have been exactly the same, and it continued in South Africa.

But I'm sure that James would say that I'm in his face if I have had a good session. It's probably down to the fact that I've always had older team-mates like Niall Mackenzie, Carl Fogarty or John Kocinski, who I've respected. And I'm sure that they would say that I was always in their faces. James is seven years younger than I am, even though he has an incredibly old head for those young shoulders. Most of the time, I just assume he's the same age as me but it has taken a bit of time to get used to the fact that he is actually so much younger.

We started to get on a lot more with each other in Australia and already this weekend we've been working better as a team, testing different parts of the bike. The bottom line is that he's a really nice lad and, taking into account his result in Valencia and the fact that he was 20th today on a track that he doesn't know, you have to say that he's a real talent. I just hope that we get on as well for the rest of the season as we have on this trip. When you are in each other's pockets for so much of the year, it can be a test of the best of friendships. If you can end the season and still really like your team-mate, you've done really well. That's only happened on a couple of occasions, with Mackenzie and Troy Bayliss, and it won't be easy, because I'm a naturally moody person, although generally not with people I respect so he has to continue to earn that!

Saturday, 28 April 2001

I had to start today's qualifying session on an English tyre, which bugged me. We did not have enough to keep putting them in throughout the weekend. And we didn't have enough of the right front tyres either, so I also had to start the session on a harder front compound than I'd been using yesterday.

'Do we not have enough?' I asked Stewart.

'No, there's nothing we can do,' he replied.

Dunlop only bring a certain amount over and allocate them to the various teams using their tyres. If, for instance, Bostrom turned round tonight and said that he was not going to use the Japanese tyre, then we'd be able to use their allocation. But if they didn't make up their mind until tonight, which was likely, then Dunlop would have to stick to their promises and share them round. It just seemed a bit strange that, in Japan, we couldn't get our hands on enough of the Japanese-made tyres.

It was pretty difficult to motivate myself for the first few laps, knowing that I would be half a second down on the times that I'd been doing yesterday. At the same time, I was trying to assess changes to the bike and what with continually switching tyres, it was really difficult. Then, just to make matters worse, the clutch problem was back. So I pulled in and said:

'Look, this is pointless. Can we not just use the Japanese tyre in bike two and get on with it?'

So that's what happened but, by now, I was a bit paranoid about not qualifying for Superpole. Troy Bayliss had missed out, so my fears were justified. Towards the end of the session we stuck on a couple of qualifying tyres and I jumped up to eighth fastest, which I was reasonably pleased with. But, on my one big flying lap, I would have bettered that time had Austrian rider Robert Ulm not crashed on the first section of the track. I was up on my second split time when the red flag came out, stopping me

70

from finishing the lap. There were only two minutes left in the session, so there was not that much point in going out again. That wasn't the case for Bayliss, though, because he was still outside the top 16. He had one chance to put in a better time, along with a few others who were queuing to get out of pit-lane when the session resumed. That must have been one of the first times that a rider leading the championship didn't qualify for Superpole. Out of that bunch, only Edwards actually put in a faster time.

For Superpole warm-up, we wanted to get rid of the 'chatter' that I'd been experiencing from the front and the rear. To do that we tried different bike lengths. Sometimes it can help if you shorten the wheelbase. But, and don't ask me why except that it's something to do with the gearing, we could only shorten it by 15mms. That doesn't sound like a lot, but it is. In fact, 5mms would normally be a lot. The first change made the bike too nervous and even created more 'chatter', if anything. However, I was still running the harder tyre in the front at this stage. It was only right at the end of the session, when I put the really soft 747 front tyre in, that most of the 'chatter' was eliminated. All along it had probably been down to the tyre more than the bike length, but these are the things you have to work out in such a short period of time. I finished that session on a qualifier and with the fifth fastest time, behind Tamada – now widely referred to as 'Cheese And' – Izutsu, Edwards and Corser.

When I saw the first two riders go out for Superpole, I absolutely shit myself. Yanagawa went first and did a 1:29.775, which was half a second than faster he had done all weekend. Bostrom then turned in a 1:29.510, which was three quarters of a second better than his previous best. 'I'm going to be 16th at this rate,' I thought.

I set myself a target of a 1:29.6 lap and my actual time was 1:29.634. To this point, I hadn't done too well round the first section of the track. But, on this lap I got the first couple of turns right and then, going into turn three – a downhill, bumpy corner where I've crashed before – I started to lose the front. That can sometimes happen with a qualifying tyre in the rear because it exaggerates the grip at the back. I stuck my knee down to save it and touched the throttle and, thankfully, the bike came back. At the same time I was glad it had happened because, instantly, the adrenaline was surging. Maybe too much, because I went too fast into the next corner. I then got my rhythm back apart from a small slide coming out of the chicane which caused me to get off the throttle and probably cost me a tenth of a second and a front row place.

I was second behind Bostrom at that stage and, when you are waiting for the others to finish, you can't help but be nasty and want them to make mistakes. Don't get me wrong, there's no way that I'd want someone to hurt themself, it's just the competitive streak in me. I eventually qualified sixth on the grid.

Before returning to the hotel I had time for a massage at the Clinica Mobile. I do seem to pay more attention to this than other riders because my muscles get tight when they are fatigued. The mechanics are busy fine-tuning my bike, but it's easy to forget that my body needs tuning. I also do more stretching than the other riders while I am on the grid before the race. That routine gives me peace of mind and I think it makes me more relaxed on the bike. Other riders, like Carl Fogarty, who don't pay too much attention to fitness, might be more naturally relaxed and can hang effortlessly off the bike. I seem to hold my body more rigidly during a race, so I feel that I need to be that bit more fit and flexible. That's my theory, anyway.

On the way back to Sendai we picked up an English fan that Darrell recognised and who had missed his bus. It absolutely amazes me that people can afford to come all this way to watch a bike race. But he had travelled all over the world watching English riders. There was another guy who sat, all on his own, opposite the garage in the grandstand all weekend with a flag that read 'British riders are best.' Another bloke called Derek, (who works for Darrell), together with his wife Esther, who looks after the hospitality for the European rounds, had made the weekend into a bit of a holiday, so we all went back for dinner back at the Italian. Typically, in Japan, it had gone from being great one night, to terrible service the next. There was just no way we could get through to the manager what we wanted. At a lot of restaurants here, there are plastic models of the dishes on view in the window – but of course, not at this one!

Sunday, 29 April 2001

'Hello,' I grunted, not really knowing what country I was in, let alone what time it was. At first I had thought the phone was the alarm … until I saw the time.

'Hiya, it's me,' said Kathryn excitedly.

'It's 6.45am. I don't need to be awake for another hour.'

'Oh, right. I've got my times wrong. I thought you'd be on your way to the circuit. I've had a really good day. I've bought my wedding dress and picked up the ring,' she continued regardlessly.

I'd actually had a terrible night's sleep as well, but the wedding is a big thing for both of us and, knowing how much it means to Kathryn, I didn't want to make a big issue of the timing of her call.

'Oh, great, tell me all about it,' I said, trying to summon up as much enthusiasm as I could on the morning – early morning – of a race.

It must have been a morning for bad timekeeping because Derek and Esther were not at the hotel on time for a lift up to the track. There was not even any discussion about whether we should wait for them, as everyone knew that I'd want to be away bang on time. They would have to spend a few million yen on a taxi. The drive up to the track provided a good chance just to get my thoughts together, cut off from the chatter in the bus by a walkman.

I didn't have a bad warm-up, putting in high 1:30 laps and a few 1:31s, with the bike feeling fine. But then my bubble was burst when I found out that Edwards had been putting in consistent 1:29 laps. I hadn't even considered the fact that he might be a threat and it appeared that he'd kept something up his sleeve. I was also a bit concerned that my groin felt tight. When I was getting changed in the garage, James kept asking:

'What's up? What's up, mate?'

'Nowt's up,' I snapped. It was one of those moments when I just wanted a bit of space.

I didn't have much space going into the first corner after yet another bad start. I put it down to our technician, Roberto, telling me not to blip the throttle as I always had done. There were too many things going on in my head, instead of concentrating on the lights with the clutch on biting point and relying on my own reactions.

The first corner at Sugo is horrible and tight and, while you know it's a place where you can make up places, it's so easy for your race to be over in the blink of an eye. When your luck's not going for you, you can rest assured that you'll be the one to go down, so I was nowhere near aggressive enough going into the first couple of corners and, by the end of the first lap, I was still down in tenth.

This is also a difficult track for passing people. It is a one-line track and the two real chances to pass are at the end of the straights. It took me a good few laps to go past Regis Laconi. He was slow in a few sections but his Aprilia is a missile, and it was only then that I felt as though I was getting into a rhythm, as I went past Bostrom and Edwards. Next in my sights was Gregorio Lavilla, who maintained a two-second gap for a while. He was also difficult to pass, because he was good out of the corners and onto the straights, so it was difficult to get into his slipstream. Riders are also intelligent; he knew to brake very late into the two places where I might have had him. It didn't matter that he didn't have corner speed because all he had to do was stop the bike mid-corner to know that I wouldn't be getting through.

Eventually, I got him on the 22nd lap of 25. It was a bit of a lunge, at the bottom of the main straight on the brakes. But the previous 10 laps, when I had been chasing Lavilla had become very tense and had taken it out of me. I felt tired and, with five laps to go, I had got a lot of 'arm-pump' in my throttle hand. I've suffered from this problem before and needed an operation two years ago to try and sort it out by cutting the bag around the muscle to try and create more space in which it can expand. It basically means that your hand will not react with the same speed and force as at the start of a race. And it meant that pulling the brake in was really difficult.

Even though I pulled away from Lavilla, I tensed up even more. As I started my last lap I had +0.4 on my board. But that was one lap old and Lavilla was right behind me, which I didn't know. Then, when I was going down the straight, I got a false neutral. I was in third gear but as I moved up to fourth I didn't hit the gear lever cleanly enough and lost all my drive. That was enough for him to get right up close and, because I wasn't concentrating on defending my line, he came alongside me and just squeezed up the inside. He ran wide and I just managed to get back underneath him but, with the next corner being a left-hander and me being on the outside, there was no way I could make it stick.

It was a massive disappointment that I'd finished seventh instead of sixth, with just Corser of the championship regulars ahead of us. It felt like I had lost the race and that everything that I'd worked for during the race had been taken away. Back in the garage, everyone was really chuffed but I was a Billy Longface. The only thing that cheered me up was hearing that James had been 11th, ahead of Edwards and Bayliss. I didn't want to be a misery-guts when everyone else seemed on a high so I made myself snap out of it.

I went straight to the Clinica Mobile to see if they could do anything about my arm. They wanted to give me an injection, but I disagreed because I knew that it could be massaged out. Injections can mask a problem instead of fixing it. They also gave me an anti-inflammatory to take 40 minutes before the race.

Jamie Whitham also came round for a chat after his race, in which he had broken down because of an electrical fault – his third DNF in three races. But he is absolutely brilliant for keeping a positive outlook and he gave me some good advice about my arm. He'd noticed that I was even tense when I was going down the straights.

'You don't need to be gripping the bars down the straights, because you're not using them. Take that chance to relax your grip and give your arm a bit of a break. Hold them like you'd tweak a woman's nipples,' he said, in typical Whitham style.

It was something that I already knew, but it never does any harm to have it drummed into you. Colin had also spent about 40 minutes analysing the timesheets from the first race and had worked out that I'd lost four seconds on the first lap to Corser, who led at the end of that lap and was eventually second behind Tamada.

'You've got to get a better start, Neil,' he said.

'You don't say, Colin,' I replied.

'I've looked at the times and, if you can do every lap in the 30s, and not drift into the 31s, you'll be right up there,' he added.

'You don't say, Colin!'

It was unusual for him to state the obvious, because he normally brings up something that I haven't considered. But, as it turned out, I did exactly what he had told me to do. My start was much better and, at the end of the first lap, I was lying sixth. A couple of laps later I tried to take Shinichi Ito, but the pass was never really on. Still, I tried to go underneath him and, when he closed back in on me, his back end just clipped my front wheel. That lifted me up and I expected three or four riders to come through on me. I quickly wobbled back into the racing line, probably messing everyone else up but by then, the group ahead had gained a couple of seconds on me.

It was just a case of getting my head down and trying to close in on Corser, who was now in sixth. From that second lap onwards I didn't come out of the 1:30s, riding as hard as I could but trying to stay relaxed on the bike. On the 17th lap, I had a bit of a moment on turn three. Corser got further away, while Bostrom had pulled a lead on him. I was three seconds up on Chili and I said to myself 'I'll take this!'

'No I bloody well won't. What are you talking about, Neil? Come on, keep fighting. That's the only way you'll be pleased with your self when the race is over. Keep pushing, you never know. Yeah, you could ease up and do lap times half a second slower. But that would be a piece of piss. You're better than that. Keep 100 per cent concentration and effort,' I raged at myself.

In all probability, though, no matter how hard I tried I was not going to catch Corser because he was very good in most parts of the track. But I was also good in two sections, at the end of the straight and into the chicane, and I could pull 20 yards on him there. That kept me in the race with him. He would pull away during the lap and then, with a big handful of brake, I would close back in at the end of the straight.

But, on the 22nd lap, he missed a gear coming out of the chicane when he was five yards in front. Instead of him pulling away as normal, I was right behind him on the straight and I knew he wasn't too good on the brakes going into the first corner. I was puffing and panting by then, as I knew this was last chance saloon to catch him. And I did. I then put two good laps together and pulled away to create a gap of 1.4 seconds at the start of the last lap.

Whitham's theory of not hanging on for all I was worth went right out the window. I was gripping the bike like a lunatic. That fifth place felt like a race win, I could really pat myself on the back because I knew I'd done everything possible. Tamada won the second race as easily as he had the first. But, when you took the wild cards out of the equation, I was effectively second behind Bostrom. Sure, it would have been nice to have been on the podium and tasting champagne, but at least it doesn't feel like that taste is going to be too far away now.

There were massive traffic jams stretching from the track and back into Sendai but Troy managed to find a short cut through some paddy fields. Back at my hotel room, a note had been pushed through the door. It was from Mary Anne Hobbs. Their flight must have been today, so they had come all this way only to miss the races. Yesterday she had bet me £50 that Tamada would not win a race. At least she promised to pay up, for what must be the easiest £100 I've ever earned. Rather than enjoy our last night in Japan, everyone was pretty exhausted and, with the prospect of an early morning train ride back to Tokyo and then onto the airport before a long flight home, an early night seemed the sensible option.

Monza – round 5

Thursday, 10 May 2001

Arrived here on the outskirts of Milan last night to find that they've totally wrecked this track. The first corner used to be bad enough but now they have made it into a complete bottleneck that goes into an unbelievably tight chicane. The old chicane used to be awesome. It was almost two chicanes in one, where the bike went left-right-left-right. Now, at the end of the straight, you brake in a straight line for a really tight right-hander, followed by an even tighter left before accelerating for the very fast Curva Grande turn two. They have also tightened up the second chicane and God knows why they had to do that because it always used to be very tight anyway. It's such a downer, especially at a track that I was looking forward to racing at again. It's the third oldest track in the world and the place has a real atmosphere. It's also set in the middle of a huge, beautiful park, which adds to the appeal of the place, and riding a Ducati in Italy always assures you of a passionate support from the locals.

The word around the paddock is that the changes have all been made for the benefit of the Formula One drivers' safety. Maybe it will be better for the spectators as well, but it would appear that our concerns are way down the pecking order and the only thing that bothers us is our own safety. A few of the riders talked today about how we would deal with the first corner and I came up with the best idea.

'Why don't we start on the back straight, so that the Parabolica is the first corner?' I suggested. The other riders agreed but the organizers said that it would be impossible from a practical point of view, with regard to erecting the traffic lights, painting the new markings and providing TV and spectator facilities.

This was the first meeting for Peter Ingley, the guy that Corser had put forward as a possible representative for the riders. I already knew him from 1993, when I was using Yokohama tyres and he was working for them. He has a long history in motor sport and used to be the top man at Dunlop so he seems to be a well-respected guy in the paddock. I think that he can only help. At a race weekend our only priority is to get a bike around the track as quickly as possible. When problems do crop up, there are not enough hours in the day to have meeting after meeting with the organizers. So we do need a representative to do that for us and it's obviously better for me that it's someone who speaks English.

'If there's anyone who disagrees with his appointment, you'd better say so now,' I said after a show of hands seemed to indicate that it was a unanimous decision.

His effect had been immediate. When we first arrived they had erected a big tyre wall with airbags, to stop riders from cutting across the first chicane. But, if you lost the front as you went into the first apex, you would crash straight into that wall and hurt yourself badly. The organisers argued that if someone did now go straight across, they would run directly into the traffic. Peter argued that there was only a five per cent chance of that happening compared to a 95 per cent chance of serious injury because of the lack of run-off. So the wall is to be removed before tomorrow's first practice session.

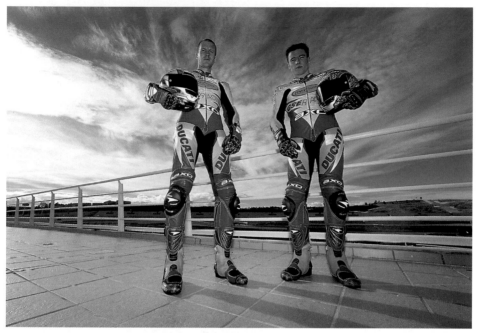

James and me doing promotional shots for the first round in Spain. It does look a bit cheesy though.

Life in the motorhome ... Kathryn washing up while I prepare my race visors for the Valencia meeting.

ROUND 2: KYALAMI

On my way to 4th place at
Kyalami in race 2.

Fully focused in South Africa.
However, I was forced to retire
with engine trouble in the first
race.

Breaking the lap record during winter testing at Kyalami.

Before the cancelled second race at Phillip Island, discussing the conditions with Colin in the garage.

Making the most of a rare dry track during the Phillip Island race weekend.

Battling against the winds at this unpredictable coastal circuit.

ROUND 4: SUGO

The unforgettable Mary Anne Hobbs, just about to talk herself out of £100.

Coming up to the start-finish straight in Japan.

The GSE geisha girls at Sugo.

Coming out of the new first corner at Monza, battling to keep the front wheel down.

Me teaching James all I know during the morning warm up.

One of the many breakdowns during a disappointing round.

An overhead shot of me negotiating the famous Parabolica at Monza.

ROUND 6: DONINGTON

Outbreaking Colin Edwards into Redgate in the 1st race at Donington ... and then celebrating my win.

Enjoying my race 1 victory, this time on the podium.

ROUND 7: EUROSPEEDWAY LAUSITZ

Getting ready to race on my way to second place ...

... the new circuit was extremely slippery in the wet.

ROUND 8: MISANO

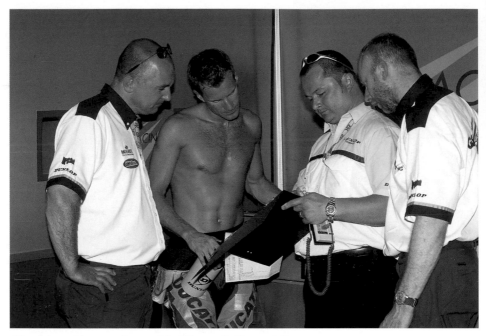

Checking the tyre data with Higgy, Colin and Stewart.

On the line for Superpole at Misano, before taking one of my four pole positions.

That's not the only change that will have to be made, as far as I'm concerned anyway. After walking round the new layout with Stewart we agreed that there's no way that first gear, as it stands on my bike, is going to be anywhere near low enough. That's going to mean some alterations straight away in order to get some drive out of there.

Friday, 11 May 2001

I'd come into this meeting full of confidence and in pretty good spirits. Back home in the Isle of Man, a really good bloke called Juan had allowed Dougie Lampkin and myself to use some fields for motocrossing. They hadn't been used for cattle and were not intended to be for the next 10 years so the Government allowed us to ride our motocross bikes there for a couple of nights, despite the foot-and-mouth restrictions. Being able to motocross always made me the happiest man in the world, but the early signs were that the rest of this particular weekend might not be such plain sailing.

For a start, this morning's first session was wet, which you don't really expect in Italy. But, after a few laps, I realised that the race line was drying. I came back in to put an intermediate tyre on the rear, keeping a wet weather tyre in the front. A few laps later and the track had dried even further, so I went back out on slicks at both the front and back. For the next five or six laps I went faster and faster until suddenly, as I crossed the start-finish line, there was an explosion from the engine. Thinking it had blown, I immediately grabbed the clutch because coming from a two-stroke background, your first concern is that the back wheel is going to lock and throw you over the bars. I moved straight off the racing line in case I was spraying oil out of the back. The danger, after pulling the clutch in, is to think that you are automatically going slowly. However, when the generator failed, I was doing 170mph so I had to slow down before pulling onto the wet grass or it could have been pretty painful. I tootled further on down the straight and pulled onto the grass. There were 12 minutes of the session remaining but I was on the wrong side of the track and the marshalls wouldn't let me cross over. So that was the end of that session. I wasn't too downhearted though because, at the time of the problem, I was the fastest and only dropped down to fifth because of the problem.

The fact that I'd missed those last few minutes in the morning on a drying track meant that I was playing catch-up to some extent. after only four laps in the afternoon I'd knocked nearly two seconds off my best time of the morning. Then, as I went into the Ascari chicane, my foot slipped on the footpeg.

'That could be oil,' I thought, as I turned to the right at 100mph. The back end whipped round, which confirmed the oil suspicion, but luckily I wasn't thrown off. I rode straight into the gravel, parked up and sure enough, the engine was smoking. A nipple that serves as a connection for an oil pipe had broken off – one of those freak things that nobody will ever get to the bottom of. I've never had one go before and I hope I'll never have one go again. The main thing was that I'd stayed on the bike, which was a real stroke of luck.

I got a lift back to the garage on a scooter and jumped onto my spare bike. This time it felt just as good as the number one bike – I couldn't tell the difference between them. I'd missed another 13 minutes of the session but managed to get my time down to 1:50.869. Then, when we threw a qualifyer on right at the end, my final lap was 1:49.748 and fourth fastest, which was not a bad result considering the circumstances.

Ducati had organised a signing session at a shop in a square in the centre of Monza on Friday evening, which I could have done without. It wasn't well organised but I had a bit of a crack with the other riders, Bostrom, Ruben Xaus, Vito Gaureschi and James in the van on the way back. It meant that I was starving by the time we got back to the affluent suburb of Monza, which is a good 45-minute drive away from the city centre at that time of night when the traffic is very heavy.

Having missed dinner with the GSE team, I went to the Ducati hospitality to eat. There was a guy there called Andrew Porter, who I knew had been involved with MB4U, sponsors of the British championships last year. I didn't particularly get on with the guy but, being polite, I asked him what he was up to.

'I'm solely with TFR,' he said.

'That means nothing to me. What is it?' I asked.

'Team Foggy Racing,' he replied with a bit of a frown that suggested I was completely stupid.

I'd heard rumours that he was fronting Carl Fogarty's attempts to set up his own team, although I had no idea it was being referred to as TFR.

'I've heard that you're interested in riding for us. Can we talk now?' he asked.

I nearly choked on my dinner. Not only was James standing less than a metre away, I was standing in the middle of the Ducati hospitality, with all their main men and quite a few journalists floating around, and here was this guy trying to get me to break my two-year deal with GSE Racing. I felt very uncomfortable and thought 'Please don't say anything else, because people are going to hear and I don't know what to say.'

'I'm sorry, I've got to dash,' I said, before scarpering pretty sharpish.

Of course I'm always interested what people have to offer, especially as it's not even certain that GSE will have a team next year if Darrell can't find any sponsorship. I had heard that Fogarty would be keen to get me on board if he was able to set up his own team. However, there is so much water to pass under the bridge before then, that it was pointless even thinking about it at this stage, let alone holding a meeting in the worst place imaginable.

Saturday, 12 May 2001

Everything seemed okay this morning when I went out for the second qualifying session, but I should have started to realise by now that this weekend was not going to plan. Sure enough, after just two laps, I felt something on my shinbone and discovered that the engine bolt had come out. This has happened before and is becoming a bit of a problem. The team do try to Loctite them in, but they still work their way out. Don't ask me how it can already have happened on three occasions at this early stage of the season, but it's perhaps a question that I should now be asking the team. I tried to kick it back into place but, instead, hoofed it out. All I could do was ride round and return to the garage, where another few minutes were wasted sorting that problem out.

Then, after one more lap and at the same sort of position where I'd had my problem yesterday afternoon, there was a similar noise from the engine and the bike started to decelerate quickly. I grabbed the clutch quickly again but I'd learned something from yesterday. This was right at the start of the session and I couldn't afford to be stranded on the left-hand side of the track again, so I drifted over to the right-hand side. It was a bit of a dangerous move because there were a lot of bikes around, practising their slipstreaming, and I didn't know for sure whether I was leaking oil.

Having parked the bike at the first corner, I sprinted all the way back in my leathers and helmet under the hot Italian sun. It must have been a full kilometre – it certainly felt like it. When I got back to the garage I was a little bit stressed – to say the very least. I was really trying to stay calm but it was a struggle, especially as I was sweating like a pig on heat. So out I went on bike number two.

Four laps later, going towards the Ascari, there was a big 'Barrrrrrrgh' and the engine had seized up yet again. This was a big blow and the engine was totally wrecked after a problem with the exhaust valve. Again, all I could do was park up and start to walk the mile back to the paddock. Chris Herring, the Castrol Honda press officer, happened to be riding past and came rushing over to give me a lift back.

'There's no need to rush, Chris. I've no bike to go back to,"'I said, with 20 minutes of the session still to go. It's fair to say that I was not a happy chappy by this point and, with the session still running, I returned to my motorhome before I said anything I might regret. I knew that I was capable of finishing on the podium here if everything went to plan. But nothing was going to plan. Instead it was all going horribly wrong and I had dropped down to 11th because everyone else had improved their times from yesterday. The worst thing for people to say was: 'Never mind, your luck will change.' You feel like saying: 'Well, it hasn't fucking well changed so far, has it?'

Between sessions was the pit-lane walkabout, which was very difficult to do. I wanted to shout and swear and behave like a four-year-old, but it doesn't look too good when you have people gawping into the garage. Nor do the Italians help matters. Having just come from Japan, where the punters form an orderly queue, this place is the exact opposite. You can be trying to sign a poster when somebody else sticks a hat in the way, so that you can't carry on with the first signature. I have to take the piss out of them to keep myself entertained.

'Nice hair,' I grinned at one guy with a seriously dodgy 'barnet'. Luckily, so far, nobody has understood what I've been saying but Kathryn's convinced that I'm going to get smacked one day. Anyway, there was always the afternoon's final free practice session to look forward to.

Everything went perfectly in that session, for all of five seconds! As I was making my way down pit-lane I moved from first to second to ... burrrrrrrgh! The bloody thing had blown before I got to the end of the pit-lane.

'Fuck it! I don't care if I wreck the engine, I'm going to do a lap. If I park here then that bike is out of action for the rest of the session,' I thought. The bike just about made it back round to the garage – breakdown number five of the weekend. This was not a laughing matter.

Amazingly, the rest of the session went smoothly. When I put a qualifier in towards the end, I improved my Friday afternoon qualifying time of 1:49.748 to 1:49.273. That improved my confidence no end because at least I now knew that I could do it. I was also confident that we had found the right tyre because I was able to do 18 laps on the Japanese Dunlop from the Sugo round. It's pretty rare to use a Japanese tyre at successive rounds but the English range was not working anywhere near as well. My lap times were around 1:50 and I knew that I was not on the limit and would be able to push those to 1:49s during the race. That would be there or thereabouts for tomorrow.

There was not much of a break for me before my Superpole lap, having qualified in 11th. I didn't mind that because sometimes it's difficult to know what to do. It's difficult not to watch the screen, because you can't help being interested. But, if another rider does a good time, it can make you push that little bit too hard and cock your own lap up.

Throughout the weekend I had been quick through the first

section but had struggled around the second section, around the Lesmo Corner. During my warm-up lap I was desperately trying to concentrate on getting this section right. But, as I started my actual lap, I braked too early into the first corner. Maybe I was too concerned about braking too late, which would have been worse. I over-compensated and instead of squeezing hard on the brake into that corner, I was letting the brake go. Even so, I still managed a good first split, although it felt slow to me. That mistake had wound me up so I really attacked the other corners, that little bit harder than I otherwise would have done. When I went over the line and saw my time of 1:48.701, I knew it was respectable.

One by one, the people that I expected to go faster than me didn't manage it. Then, the one rider who I thought might put a bit of a ragged lap together, Troy Bayliss, was the man to pip me right at the death. Still, I couldn't complain with second on the grid after everything that had happened over the weekend. You also get a wadge of cash for finishing in the top three of Superpole, which is always handy.

I was now optimistic for the races, because I knew that the trouble I'd suffered all weekend couldn't continue. All I needed was a good night's sleep. But, of course, even that wasn't possible here. Aprilia were throwing a party in their hospitality unit, which was set up only 50 yards or so away from where my motorhome was parked. I could have accepted it if the band had stopped at a reasonable hour, but they carried on until nearly midnight. It is so stupid. Why do the organisers allow them to do this, knowing that 70 per cent of the riders are staying in the paddock? And how can Aprilia themselves be so selfish as not to consider the preparations of the other teams?

Sunday, 13 May 2001

I'd planned to practise a bit of slipstreaming during morning warm-up. It turned out that James and I went out together and I don't know whether James knew what my plan was, but we ended up slipstreaming and out-braking each other. If it hadn't have been him, it would have been somebody else, though. That's something that you don't do during qualifying because you are too concerned with putting in fast laps. When I returned to the garage I think the team was a bit disappointed with my times, but that was never the idea as far as I was concerned. And it should also have been taken into account that I went out with a second-hand tyre because of the shortage of the Japanese rears, but I didn't mind too much, because it was still pretty fresh.

I'm not a particularly superstitious bloke, but you get a feeling when things aren't meant to be. When Troy pulled the garage door up for the pit-lane walkabout before the first race, the first Italian guy in the queue was wearing a Blackburn Rovers shirt. And he wanted me to sign it! As a supporter of Burnley, their arch-rival, that is not what you want to see. It's probably the equivalent to running over a black cat.

Still, I managed a really good start and a good first corner, flopping into second place. All I could think about was 'Stay with them.' Monza is all about tow and, if you lose that, your race is all over. The riders I was battling with at the front all had faster bikes than mine - not by miles but worth 0.4 seconds a lap. However, even though I was riding a bit raggedly in the opening few laps, I managed to pass Troy Bayliss to take the lead – for the first time in the year.

This might sound stupid, but I didn't realise I was leading. I knew there was nobody in front of me, but at no time did I think 'Bloody hell, you're in front.' I'm pleased about that because it didn't make me unnecessarily anxious and it proves that that's where I believe I should be in a race. For a few laps it was just a case of them passing me on the straights and then me coming back past on the brakes, which my set-up allowed me to do by leaving it really late.

Ruben Xaus joined the breakaway group of Bayliss, Edwards and myself, and on lap five he moved into third place. That didn't worry me at all, because I was still in touch with them and usually the action doesn't really start until the last couple of corners. Then I turned into Ascari and, because Xaus was in front, he blocked my view slightly. I turned in too early, hit the kerb on maximum lean and the front wheel came off the ground. I heard a big scrape, which meant that the fairing had caught the ground and I was really lucky to stay on. It left me really wide on a sequence of flip-flop left-rights, left-rights, and if you are behind yourself in the first part of that section, you are behind all the way through it. As a result, I lost a bit of time there but, more importantly, I lost the tow from the leading three. It also meant that I came onto the straight too slowly so instantly, they had gained another two tenths. And all from that one mistake!

Perhaps I was even more ragged after that, because I was desperately trying to get back in touch. But there was nothing I could do about it and I thought 'This is the worst case scenario, to end up on your own.' The only pleasing thing was that I was pulling away from the group behind. All I could do was hope that the front three would slow each other down through crazy braking.

Eventually Xaus also lost the tow and ended up coming back towards me. Soon I felt that I was in control of whether I could be either right behind him, or a second behind him. He was stronger than I was in a few places, but I felt relaxed and confident that I would be able to pass him because I was stronger than he was at a few other sections. Having said that, I didn't particularly want to get into a battle with him. Ruben is a typical spaniard, he get rushes of blood to the head and can go a bit crazy. The plan was to leave any passing until the last lap, make a firm move and then do a clean lap to make it stick. The last thing I wanted was a repeat of Japan, when I'd given Lavilla a chance to look at me for a lap.

However, between laps seven and ten I'd had a problem with the gear-shifter, so the bike was jumping out of gear in weird places like round the Parabolica. All of a sudden, from a smooth throttle action, it would go 'Dup-dup-dup-dup-dup'. It wasn't going into neutral but, because it's a bumpy corner, the sensitivity of the gear lever momentarily cuts the ignition. It was perhaps even more frustrating when the problem stopped because it was so difficult to explain what had been going on at the end of the race.

On lap 15, I turned into the last corner and, with the throttle closed, the back end broke traction and came straight back. It doesn't normally do that with a closed throttle. So my immediate thought was 'Oil!' I looked over my shoulder and couldn't see anything wrong. As I tipped it into the first corner, at the end of the start-finish straight, I knew my race was over. The bike slid and gripped and this time, when I looked over my shoulder, all I could see was white smoke.

'Not again,' I thought, with all emotion draining out of my body. All I could do was pull into the side of the track, park up but what I wanted to do was go and lie down somewhere – preferably on the track so that I could stop the race! It's not a physical track but my spirit was broken. To add insult to injury, while I stood there and watched them come round again, Xaus was no longer there. He had fallen off, which would have handed me a certain third place. Maybe I should be thankful for small mercies – that he didn't crash before I broke down. I also felt deflated for the team, because I know how personally Stewart takes everything, and, with another engine problem, he would be mortified. Perhaps other riders would think 'Those bastards, it's all their fault' in similar circumstances.

It didn't help matters when the marshalls started laughing and saying:

'Ah, Hodgson! Yesterday, two bikes. Today this!'

'Yes, Ducati shit!' I joked, trying to make conversation. It was the biggest mistake of my motorcycling career. Their faces turned to thunder.

'No, no, no, no, no,' shouted one of the marshalls. I thought I was going to be lynched because, suddenly a gang of people all wearing orange were marching towards me. I didn't think they were going to punch me but they were certainly not very happy. I'd said something that was clearly not allowed.

'Joking, joking! Ducati numero uno,' I insisted.

They must have believed me because they helped me haul the bike into the truck and gave me a lift back to the garage. Colin was waiting, he quickly closed the shutter and then ordered everyone out while he found out what had happened. I then spent the break between races back in the motorhome, watching the British Superbike championship races from Oulton Park, looking forward to the second race because I now knew that I could run with them as long as the bike was functioning.

For the first time in a long time I crept forward at the start, ever so slightly. You are probably only allowed about three inches before it's deemed a jump start. I hadn't meant to roll, of course. It just started to go as I was trying to find the biting point for the clutch. And I really panicked. The red light seemed like it had been on for two seconds so, instead of braking, I carried on letting it go. Half a second later when it still hadn't gone out, I had to touch my brake or it would definitely have been a jump start and, of course, as soon as I touched my brake the red light went out. I had lost all my rhythm but managed to claw a few places back up to fifth with a really good first corner.

The plan was the same as for the first race, just to stay with the leading pack. But, on every single straight, I was being passed by at least one rider. And they weren't creeping past, they were flying past, which was really disconcerting. I couldn't even get back in their slipstream and pass them at the next corner. Slowly I was working my way back through the field.

At the end of lap four I was ninth and, two laps later, the bike was starting to vibrate. After what had happened over the weekend, I expected it to lock up or leak oil again. I went past Corser, who also had a problem, a couple of laps later.

'I bet he's thinking I wish I was Hodgson,' I thought. 'Little does he know!'

I was fully expecting to be pulling in at any time, but there was no way I was going to quit and the bike continued to the end. With two laps remaining, I even managed to pass Regis Laconi to move into seventh place, but I was spitting mad. As far as I was concerned this was effectively my seventh breakdown of the weekend. It might sound like bullshit but, throughout last year, I had just one problem with my bike. So to have seven in a weekend was too much to take. It wasn't as if it was the same thing. This latest one turned out to be a faulty valve and the rest had not been related to each other.

It felt like I was riding round with a big sign saying: 'Look at me! I'm Neil Hodgson, not performing again like you all said I would.' People might not be thinking that, but that's what it feels like. It's worse than crashing, because all this is out of my hands. I was perhaps a bit stroppy with my mechanics in the holding bay – not effing and blinding – but stressing the fact that there had been another major problem. They probably feel as bad as I do but I needed them to know straight away why I was only seventh.

Ducati have been really good with their support but, because none of these problems were the fault of my mechanics – like Pete forgetting to tie the clip on or Dave forgetting to put oil in the engine – you then have to look at the cause of the problems. Problems with the ignition and valves are problems with the bike. You also have to bear in mind that we are running second hand parts, as this bike is a year old. So you couldn't help feel that if these parts were replaced, this kind of disastrous weekend could be avoided in the future.

Soon after the race Colin came to tell me that Ducati had agreed to replace everything free of charge. Obviously they had taken the view that to have one of their bikes breaking down so often at one race meeting was not a good advertisement for the company, even though Bayliss had gone on to win both races. More than anything, I was happy for the mechanics. They deserved better than the luck we'd had this weekend.

I feel like I am riding well and perhaps everything was made worse this weekend by the fact that I knew I was capable of winning there. Compare that to somewhere like Phillip Island, where a realistic aim had been to get on the podium. My expectations had been shattered here and it was very hard to accept.

You can sit and calculate things until the cows come home, and that has perhaps been a fault in the past. I am eighth in the championship after five rounds, already 92 points behind Bayliss. So, with my hand on my heart, I'd now be over the moon if I could finish fourth in the championship. That would be a fantastic result, behind people like Bayliss, Edwards and Corser, after such a poor start. The only way to do that, though, is to be a regular podium finisher from now on in – and to also get some wins. Hopefully, the next round at Donington might provide that lift.

Donington – round 6

Thursday, 24 May 2001

I woke up on the Tuesday after the Monza races feeling like a big, dark cloud was hovering over the bed. The Monday had not been too bad, because we were travelling back home and that took my mind off things, but the weekend's events really caught up with me the following day.

'Are you all right, Neil?' asked Kathryn.

'No, I'm bloody miserable,' I snapped.

It took until the Wednesday afternoon, when I went to the gym, to clear the cloud away and then I had to throw myself into a few other engagements, which also provided a welcome distraction. I spent a day trying to keep warm at the big SED trade show for bulldozers, excavators and diggers, having turned up in T-shirt and jeans on a foul day. It was a good day to say thank you to John Jones, the head of HM Plant, one of our main sponsors. I've been involved with lots of team sponsors down the years but he's the best by a mile. Some you can't really relate to and it's clear they are just there for their own business interests. John knows the right moments to talk to you and the right times to leave you alone. He's a self-made man – a typical happy-go-lucky Geordie really – and his wife Kath is just as enthusiastic about the racing.

After spending a night at Darrell's house in Kent, I helped launch a bike safety video made by Kent police. The county had experienced 30 motorbiking deaths that year and the police were giving away the video to everyone buying any bike over 600cc. It included clips of me winning at Brands Hatch last year but also the story of how I nearly killed myself on the roads a few years ago.

While my friend was holiday, he'd leant me his Honda Fireblade. I'd probably only ridden on the road before on a couple of occasions but that didn't stop me thinking I was a bit special on this machine. A guy at my gym at home in Burnley, Big Tom, was always telling me how fast he went riding with his mates. So I hooked up with them and it turned out that they were actually very fast. I really struggled to stay with them on the first day, when we were riding round places like Hawes in the Lake District, where I didn't know the roads.

By the third and final day I was about the quickest there – and we were going fast. We were not even slowing down to go through villages. It's not something that I'm proud of, but it just goes to show how easily people are egged on. Not too far from home, I was third in a line of around eight bikes. The two riders in front passed two cars in one go but I hesitated slightly. I couldn't see enough ahead of me but still thought 'Go for it' because you can go past cars so quickly on these bikes. When I got out into the middle of the road a car came round the corner in front of me very quickly.

Talk about time standing still! I had a quick decision to make: Should I accelerate and just squeeze into the gap, stay where I was and hit the car head on, brake hard and squeeze back into where I'd just pulled out of, or kill a bit of speed and crash into the trees. Luckily the guy driving the car in front looked in his mirror, saw that I wasn't going to make it and did an emergency stop. It saved my life. If he had carried on at normal speed there's no way that I'd have been able to get back in behind him.

With the front and back brakes on, the bike slid round the corner but just managed to avoid the oncoming car. It was one of the worst feelings I've ever had on a bike. I've ridden them all my life and have never been so scared. Five miles further on we parked up at my mate's house in Burnley and I was as white as a sheet.

'You don't know how close I was to dying back there,' I said to them. 'And if you carry on riding like that for 10 years there's no doubt that you will die – the time is ticking. You might as well be riding in the TT.' To prove the point one of the guys I was out with on that day crashed soon afterwards, went under a car and is now brain-damaged. I still see him at my gym and Big Tom, who roped me into the ride in the first place, also crashed last year. He doesn't ride anywhere near as quickly now.

'Have I told you about my crash?' he asks me every time I see him.

'Have I told you about my hundred crashes? Welcome to the real world. Anyone can ride a bike fast but it's how fast you ride it after you've hit the tarmac,' I laugh at him.

After the video launch, I had to catch a plane back to the Isle of Man. However, it was teatime in Kent and I had the M25 to negotiate, so I got in the back of a police car with a couple of middle-aged coppers and we had a really good laugh, tearing along the back roads. I loved it, because I'm a big kid at heart and they also let me in on a few trade secrets. Then, when they dropped me off outside departures at Gatwick, one wound his window down, waited until I had got out with my bags, and shouted:

'Right, this is your last warning. If we catch you bumming men again you're in big trouble.' I didn't know where to put myself.

The next night – Saturday – I was just getting ready for bed when the phone went at 11pm. It was David Jefferies, who I've known since the age of 13 when we competed against each other at motocross. He's had a fantastic few years at the TT, winning three races last year but has had a lot of bad luck with teams. He was supposed to be doing British Superbikes this year but his team fell through at the last minute so he has ended up in the Production Class. Dave was over on the island doing a piece for a magazine about the 'TT That Never Was', and was out with John McGuinness, a former British 250cc champion and a winner of the ultra-lightweight TT. You know who your mates are when they only ring you at 11pm on their big night out, so I gave Dave a bit of a tongue-in-cheek mouthful. I then spent a couple of days relaxing before what was always going to be a mad weekend for me. I actually got into a book, which is very rare for me. but Lance Armstrong's *It's Not About The Bike* is just about the best book I've ever read and I found it very inspirational.

On Wednesday night I travelled back over to the mainland, in preparation for the morning's pre-race press conference at a hotel outside Derby, where the England football team were also staying before their game against Mexico on Saturday night. I was a bit annoyed that the timing of the conference, 8.30 in the morning, meant that I had to travel a day early. So you can imagine how I felt when the thing didn't get underway until 9.30am, meaning that I could have travelled that same morning. I realise that these events are part of the job, but I don't think people realise how much you put yourself out sometimes. It left me with a couple of hours to go back to the track and wash my motorhome before returning to the hotel for a lunch with journalists organised by Octagon, the people who own World Superbikes with Flammini. There was someone there from *The*

Times and *The Sun*, although you are never sure whether to trust those papers' reporters fully.

By the time I was back at Donington for 4pm, I'd not even seen the team and was already thinking 'enough's enough – too many interviews already. I want to concentrate on the riding now.' But in the evening, after dinner with the team, we took the chance to drive 10 minutes to the home of Charlie and Julie Cash, who ran the physiotherapy clinic for the British championship. I'd seen them a lot throughout last season for massages and general physiotherapy treatment and it was good to catch up – and have a full body massage.

Friday, 25 May 2001

Stewart had made a few alterations to the engine and all the new parts that Ducati had promised were now in the bike, so I did a couple of laps before coming in again to check that everything was working okay. Then I tried to stay out for as long as possible because Donington is a technical old track and you need to get dialled in to it as quickly as possible. I was on it straight away. I ended the session the quickest, with two wild cards, Steve Hislop and John Reynolds, second and third. Ideally that would be the perfect situation for the races, so that I could pull some points back on the guys ahead of me in the championship. The British lads were not that far behind, though, with Hislop lapping at 1:34.361 compared to my 1:34.119.

I hadn't dared to think about the races before arriving here. But, once I had been on the bike to make sure that all the changes had worked okay, I could now start dreaming of two race wins on Sunday. It also looked as though everyone else was struggling. Had I come here and been down in fourth or fifth, I wouldn't have known what to think.

That could never have been the case, though, because I do know Donington. I know the lines, the pit-falls, a few wallows and bumps, so I know how the bike should feel round here. It was nice in the first hour to know that we were right in the ballpark as far as set-up was concerned. I'd tried three tyres and found one good one, which I thought would turn out to be the race tyre – a 747 English compound. But the plan for the afternoon was to try the Japanese tyre that I'd used at the last two rounds. It felt slightly better but, again, we only had four tyres and couldn't waste any.

'If you think that's going to be the race tyre, we'll have to save it until Superpole warm-up,' said Colin.

Ideally, I'd be setting off in qualifying sessions with a full tank and the race tyres on. But, for Dunlop to bring enough to make sure all the riders got exactly what they wanted throughout the weekend, they'd probably have to double or even treble their stock. We also altered the offset angle to make it steeper. So, on maximum lean, the bike would turn on a sharper radius, which helps at a few fast corners like Craner Curves, where it was running wide. It was a bit similar to Japan, where all the changes that we made seemed to work.

Another thing we tinkered with was the gearing because I wanted slightly fewer revs everywhere as it was a little bit 'peaky' in places. The only other slight change was to the mapping as the power was good everywhere except the Melbourne Loop and Goddards, two tight first gear corners. When I turned the throttle there was initially nothing there, but then a sudden bang. When that happens it's really difficult to keep the bike smooth like a tractor all the way through the corner. There is no guarantee that changes like that are going to work perfectly, but this was spot on.

I'd been fastest again through most of the session and was

very surprised to see Steve Hislop beat my best time towards the end of the session. I was mad, not at Steve, but because I'd put a qualifier in which felt terrible – even worse than the race tyre.

'That qualifier is useless,' I said, with a few minutes remaining.

'Well, we've got a development tyre that no one has ever used,' said Higgy, our Dunlop technician.

'Is it a qualifier?' I asked.

'Yeah, definitely. But it's a totally different construction to anything you've had before,' he added.

So, as I was going down the pit-lane, I was thinking 'Hang on a minute. This round is important to me. I'm going out on something that no one has ever tried before. Is it going to work? Or is it going to throw me over the handlebars?'

I was trying to talk myself into really going for it and turning the throttle early. After a couple of corners I gave it a big handful – and had a big slide. Then when I caught a back-marker, I thought to myself 'This is your last lap, mate! If you want to be fastest at the end of the day you are going to have to start going some.' So I put my head down, although Steve still beat me by 0.071 of a second. I suppose it was just pride more than anything, but I felt that if I hadn't done that bad lap and on that bad tyre, I'd still have been on provisional pole.

Between sessions, I went to see a company that provides me with a car, Norton Way Honda, in their private box. I'm not blowing smoke up their backsides for the sake of it but they are a very professional bunch and delightful to work with, so it was a pleasure to sign a few posters and meet their clients. It was made clear at the start that they didn't want to keep me for any longer than they had to which was nice. At some places ou turn up and have to put up with some pissed bloke with his arm round you telling you how to ride round Redgate! Another thing John

Jones of HM Plant had arranged for this round as part of his efforts to secure a sponsor for the remainder of this season, was to paint the bike with the logo of Fiat-Hitachi. They had agreed to sponsor us for the Misano race and we thought it would be a good idea to have some pictures ready of the bike with their logo on it by that round. Hopefully they would then sponsor us for the rest of the series and maybe for next year. It looks like we've made a real effort and you can only try your best with these things, as the sponsorship market is quite fickle.

In the evening I walked around the track with Stewart. We would normally do this on a Thursday but he didn't arrive in time as he was still working on engines at his home in York. It's a great exercise for providing detailed information and, having been riding round for a day already, it was easy for him to solve little things that had been puzzling him. He might not have realised that there was a slight rise at a specific part of the track where the rear had been upset. So he'd immediately say 'You didn't tell me about that. Right, we need more damping there,' and make a little note with his pen and pad. And I always thought he was doing his shopping list. But he is so talented at realising exactly what the bike needs.

We then met up with John McGuinness, with whom I've raced motocross since I was a kid, his girlfriend Becky, Paul Bird, who runs the MonsterMob team, and his girlfriend Karen. She's the daughter of Ben Atkins, who owns the Reve Red Bull team, MonsterMob's main rivals. But this weekend Karen was supporting John Reynolds from her dad's team and not Steve Hislop from her boyfriend's team. If that was my girlfriend, I think I'd be a bit pissed off. It's an 'Either you're with me or you're not' situation. I suppose it's like our team owner, Darrell, being Troy Bayliss's manager, which is another fairly weird situation although I know that he's rooting for me!

Saturday, 26 May 2001

I have never known a day like this in my racing career. I've not stopped for one second, and at one point it all became a bit too much. The morning session went pretty smoothly, again trying a different gearing to give me just a few less revs in certain places. We also altered the clutch to give me more slip, as I was getting a lot of engine braking into the hairpin corners. It might look good with the back end sliding, but that is not the quickest way around Donington. We actually tried two different ways of doing this and it worked well on one bike, but not on the other. I'd done about 14 laps out of a total of 28 on the back-up 747 tyre before sticking in a couple of qualifiers to make sure I qualified for Superpole in as high a position as possible.

Strangely, it was the hardest qualifier, which had felt terrible yesterday, that felt much better today and that's the one I went for. However, Hislop again put in a very fast lap at the end and I was 0.442 seconds behind him with a time of 1:33.093. His lap was quicker than anything I'd ever done around here, so I had to respect that. He seems to be good around Craner Curves and the Old Hairpin, the first split, because I'd followed him around there. I go through the Old Hairpin in second, whereas he uses third gear, so I am actually quicker when the tyres have gone off slightly. That's because when I turn the throttle it goes straight to the back tyre and I've got the feel, which he won't have in third.

After morning qualifying, I was having a chat with the team in the garage. Colin told me that I had to be at the SBK tent in 15 minutes to sign some autographs. The organizers had been really good in providing me with passes for the weekend, so I did feel obliged. I jumped on my scooter and pretty well signed autographs all the way back to my motorhome to get changed. From SBK I was ushered straight to the pit-lane walkabout for another 15 minutes of constant signing.

It's the hardest thing to leave a queue of people without a signature. It must be really difficult for them to understand, but I do try to fit everything in that I'm expected to do, so sometimes, you have no choice but to be firm with people. Straight afterwards, a guy picked me up and took me to the big Ducati tent in the infield. At this point it was all starting to bug me that I'd still not had a chance to speak to Stewart about the morning's session and a few little things that I wanted to try for the afternoon.

I was with Ducati for 20 minutes, where I asked for some pasta, because I was so hungry. It was the worst pasta that I've ever had and had obviously been cooked three weeks before and left in water since then. And the bolognese sauce was from the same tin that we had at school - and I remember not liking it at school! I wouldn't have fed it to my dog, and I don't even have one. By the time I was back in my motorhome, where I'd booked a massage with Charlie, I was well and truly behind schedule and only just had enough time to get my leathers back on and go to the garage – still starving hungry because I'd not bothered with the pasta. All I'd had was a banana, a fig roll and a bit of Lucozade. That's not enough when you have been riding hard for an hour in the morning.

Within 20 minutes I was back on the bike for another 28 laps, finishing 0.013seconds behind Ruben Xaus, who had apparently been trying to tail me all day. At one point, unknown to me, he almost ran over one of his mechanics because he was so desperate to follow me out of the pits, in order that he could see where I was picking up time. At some stage in the morning I'd been conscious that someone was behind me, and I didn't do a bad lap. He was still there on the next lap, so I had a look to see who it was. Even though it was my former team-mate Troy Bayliss, I let him go past. I knew he was struggling and he knew that I liked the track. So I could have either towed him round for a couple of laps to help him out or pull over and let him sort himself out.

The plan for the afternoon was to go out on a second-hand rear tyre that I'd completed four quick laps on towards the end of the morning session. It was, therefore, a total surprise when Steve came past me by braking late at the Melbourne Loop, as that was the first time someone had gone past me all weekend. I decided to follow him for a lap and was pleased to see that he made a few mistakes. I was planning to pass him down the back straight on the brakes into the Esses. I lined it up perfectly and was determined to out-brake him, no matter what. By now there was a bit of a psychological game going on.

'If he out-brakes me here, I'm coming straight into the pits because there must be something wrong with my set-up,' I thought, knowing that there was no way I could have left it any later. So I was pretty relieved when he missed the corner altogether and ran very wide! After another lap we put the Japanese tyre in and I banged in 11 quick successive laps.

It was towards the end of that stint that I started to feel dizzy and faint because I'd not had enough to eat at lunchtime. That made me really angry because it's something that could have been avoided. I didn't feel tired, I just wasn't able to concentrate and almost felt as though I was not on the bike. That's when you break your arm, because you are not with it.

I came in to the garage and said: 'I feel dizzy.'

'Well, you should have had something to eat at lunchtime,' someone quipped. Although I knew they were joking I had to bite my lip and just sat at the back for five minutes and had a drink of water before going out on a qualifier at the end of the session.

In Superpole I managed my first 1:32 of the weekend and, if

you go faster in Superpole than you have been going all weekend, nobody can complain. I also made the most of my slowing down lap, pulling a few wheelies and doing my best ever 'stoppie' going into the Melbourne Loop. It must have lasted for 100 yards and I was well happy. I'd been doing skids going into Goddards on every slowing down lap, locking the back wheel and sliding in for a bit of fun if nobody was behind me. So I tried that again and it worked better than before.

'Oh, that feels nice,' I thought as I took my foot off the back brake. But nothing happened. The wheel continued to slide because I'd stalled the bike! Slightly embarrassing! So I pulled the clutch in and the bike came back round, allowing me to try and bump start it as I was still probably going at 40mph. No joy! Stewart later told me that I would have had to have been going at 60mph at least if it was to bump-start, because the compression had been raised.

I didn't want to mess Steve's lap up or even risk a fine, because the organizers would not have taken kindly to me cocking up the session. So I parked the bike out of the way next to some straw bales and jogged back to the garage, while the announcer Fred Clarke was taking the piss that I couldn't ride a bike. When I saw the scoreboard it said '1st – Hodgson: 1:32.899'.

'Brilliant, first pole of the year,' I thought, as the crowd cheered me back to the pit-lane. But as soon as I saw my mechanic, Pete, I knew that Hislop had gone quicker. The downside of qualifying second is that there was yet another official duty to perform, the Superpole press conference, where I told Steve that the next time I was out motocrossing with him on the Isle of Man, I'd be out to break his leg. After another spate of autographs, I was desperate to get back to the motorhome to finally have a snack. Then, without time for a shower, it was straight to a press conference that the team had arranged because we were on home turf and wanted to gain as much publicity as possible.

Back at the motorhome, Charlie was already waiting to give me my massage, which made me late for dinner. Bang on 7pm, my mobile went and it was Colin wanting to know where I was. I made it to hospitality five minutes late and it was a good job that a fine was not even mentioned – until I noticed that James wasn't there.

'Where's James,' I casually asked, doing a bit of shit-stirring.

'He's probably sulking about his fine,' said Colin.

'Why? Was he speeding in the pit-lane again?' I asked, not knowing that James had been fined 1000 Swiss Francs for turning up late for his Superpole start. The bike had failed to start on a couple of occasions in the garage, making him 43 seconds late for his lap. On the face of it, it looked as though he would have to pay the fine, so I felt I had to say something as I was still a bit annoyed that I'd had to pay for the breakdown in South Africa.

'Surely that won't come out of his pocket?' I asked.

'No, it was Baz who cocked up the start,' said Colin, as though he was working out how much each mechanic would be charged. Hopefully it was tongue-in-cheek, although Baz didn't seem to see the funny side. I had raced against Baz in 1991 and 1992 in the 125cc British championships and he was a really handy lad. He probably beat me as many times as I beat him but he was at the end of his career while I was at the start of mine. He then went on to work for Rob McElnea and Niall Mackenzie, which is how he joined GSE when Niall was my team-mate last year. Baz has a very dry sense of humour and is another real character in the team. I hope that I'll be as fit as he is when I retire, because he really looks after himself by eating a diet of just carrots!

After dinner I went to see the team for the pre-race briefing and then I had to meet another journalist back at my motorhome for a long interview. Even after that I wanted to find time to see a couple of people that I wanted to catch up with, Steve Brogan and his girlfriend, and Simon from Travelworld, from whom I'd bought my motorhome.

So the point that I want to make is that if anyone ever thinks that I'm being rude, it's not intentional. I apologise if I wasn't able to sign your autograph but that is a typical day at Donington for me. It was horrible. I intend to speak to the team at the end of this meeting to make sure the same thing doesn't happen for Brands. If just one or two engagements were cut, it would make a world of difference.

I was going to bed pretty exhausted and it didn't help that last thing at night, I saw a weather forecast that said that it was going to rain tomorrow. The possibility of rain hadn't even entered my head until that point, so I was really pissed off.

Sunday 27 May 2001

Kathryn was up at around 6am to go to the toilet and I asked her to look outside at the weather.

'It's raining,' she said.

'Oh no,' I groaned. I knew that I'd worked as hard as anyone during practice and that I'd got a good race set-up and race tyre. But the weather was throwing it all out of the window. By morning warm-up it was just spitting, so I just rode round not wanting to risk anything and just basically got used to the conditions. I could see that the track was drying quickly and although I stayed on wet tyres, I would have gone faster if I'd come back in and changed to intermediates.

When I arrived at the garage for the first race, where there was lots of media attention, I was very nervous. The track was almost dry although there was still a very fine drizzle. But, like snow, it wasn't 'sticking' on the track. On the sighting lap I could still see a couple of dark patches, but not on the racing line. As I arrived back on the start line the team were ready to change the tyres to intermediates.

'Leave them alone. Definitely. There's not even a question about it,' I said, although it was still drizzling slightly.

'If it were me, I'd use a very lightly cut slick,' said Higgy, the Dunlop guy, and I could tell that Stewart agreed.

'No way, it's definitely full slicks,' I insisted. This was my decision and I would have been gobsmacked if it had pissed it down.

Some of the other teams were in a real flap. Troy Bayliss had to start the warm-up lap from the pits because he wanted to change at the last minute and Suzuki were throwing tyres over the pit-wall because one of their riders had changed his mind at the last minute. I was convinced that the rain was not going to get any worse and that the track would stay dry. I couldn't believe that everyone else was panicking so much. Steve Hislop was next to me with slicks on, and he didn't look to be the slightest bit concerned either. Yet, to my right, Bostrom and Edwards both had cut slicks. I couldn't believe it.

When the three-minute board was shown, after which you can't change your tyres, a ray of sunlight shone down and dazzled me because I had a clear visor on.

'Your grandad's put the sun out for you,' said Kathryn, who was holding the brolly next to me. I was pretty close to my grandad Dennis, who died more than a year ago, and the thought that he was looking down on me struck a chord and made me very emotional. It also made me really determined.

It wasn't my best start but, going into the first corner, I was laughing inside my helmet. It was bone dry and I was able to bang it in, with my knee down on the floor. 'What on earth does anyone want a cut slick in for?' I thought.

'Don't try and do it all in one lap,' Fogarty had said to me as I came out of the garage. 'Take some time to settle in and you'll be fine.'

'm glad he said that because, although I was down in fifth and I knew everyone had the wrong tyres in, it made me concentrate on not doing anything stupid, and I stayed calm even though Edwards started to pull away a bit. Gradually, I passed them one by one. By lap five I was past Bayliss and into second and, although there was a bit of a gap to Edwards, I closed it in no time. 'This is going to be easy,' I thought. I passed him on lap eight, pulled a two-second lead and felt really comfortable.

Then my visor started to steam up and I lost a bit of concentration. Suddenly the gap was down by two tenths and, after the following lap, by three tenths, with Hislop now in second. 'Someone is making a charge here,' I thought, telling myself to step up the pace. I wasn't panicking, because I was already just riding round rather than racing.

By the next lap the gap was back at +5 seconds as Hislop had made a mistake and run into the grass, having gone down too many gears into the Old Hairpin. My lead was six seconds with eight laps to go. And that fact was enough to set the gremlins off.

'Don't throw this one away. Don't break down. If you do screw this one up, you'll have to retire. Remember Hockenheim, when you led Fogarty into the last corner and fucked up. This race can only be yours to mess up,' I was rambling to myself.

All this time, Steve was riding a very good race. I was his carrot and he made it back up to second from fifth place, before being pipped into second by Frankie Chili at the last turn. But those two were never a threat and, although I did run wide at a couple of corners, the race was never in doubt and I won by 2.692 seconds.

It felt nothing like the previous year, when I'd also won here. That was the best feeling of my career. Even the third place from the first race of last year felt better than this. This was more a feeling of relief. Perhaps the whole pressure of the weekend had got to me before the race. Sure, I was excited. But I'd almost been thinking about today's second race from the first corner of the first lap – I was so sure that I was going to win this one.

On my victory lap my brother and my best mate came shouting and screaming onto the track to give me a big Union Jack with my name on it. But it's a big heavy thing and when you get up to 50mph, it's a tough job just hanging onto it. So I wasn't able to pull the wheelies that I wanted to and they were a bit disappointed that I didn't say anything to them. Maybe I was just out of breath from the anxiety of the last few laps.

Being on the top step of the podium felt good but I was surprised when Chili drenched me in champagne and caught me in the eye, which really stings. Normally we don't spray each other after race one, knowing that we have to go out and race again. But I was giving this set of leathers away for a newspaper competition, so it wasn't a big problem as I had a new set for the next race.

After all the usual press commitments, I was running late again so the team cancelled an engagement that I had with our sponsors, HM Plant, arranging for me to see them after the second race. So, today, I was able to chill out at lunchtime, having some pasta and a massage from Charlie.

Despite the ease with which I'd won, the drive from the rear tyre had not felt good and I found out that I'd not been on the tyre that I'd expected. They had used the 747 instead of the Japanese tyre, thinking it would better suit the track temperature. It was a bit of a surprise that it hadn't worked too well, but it did mean that I was looking forward to the next race even more, knowing that I had a tyre to come that would give me half a second a lap.

A better start was crucial for race two, which was always going to be a different kettle of fish. All the riders were on slicks in dry conditions and I didn't want anyone to pull away early on. I kept my second place going into the first corner behind Edwards, who I expected to be the main threat as he'd been the next most consistent rider throughout practice. But I passed him on the fourth lap and built up a 1.8 second lead within another five laps. That means you've effectively cleared off and I didn't even feel like I'd put a good lap together by then. 'I've done it,' I told myself, still determined to keep attacking.

As I got on the brakes for the first corner, I went for the clutch and it had gone. The lever had no tension and was just loose and floppy. It's a problem we've had all year but this was the first time it had happened this weekend. You use the clutch to go down the gears smoothly, because to do it through engine braking would all but lock the back wheel. Letting the clutch out between gears gets round this and makes a big difference going into slow corners.

As soon as it happened, I knew what it meant. The next time I saw my board the gap was down to +1.5 and, by the next lap, it was down to +0.7. 'They are going to catch me, so I've got to try and ride round it,' I said to myself.

When Corser did finally come past he pulled away within half a lap, although I was trying so hard to stay with him. But the gap stopped growing and then I started to feel comfortable behind him. A couple of laps later, however, and he was holding me up. The fact that someone was now in front of me had put all thought of the clutch problems out of my head. As Colin Wright always says: 'Everyone else is having problems out there, so you've just got to get on with it.'

Three laps later and I was back past him and making another break of half a second, but suddenly I had something else to worry about, because Chili had overtaken Corser and was now hounding me. I didn't know which rider it was, although you can normally tell whether it's a twin-cylinder or four. I didn't even know how many bikes there were – and I didn't care.

The clutch was causing the biggest problems at the first gear corners and, with two laps to go, I braked into the Melbourne Loop at what I thought was the right time. I normally go down two gears on entering the corner and then go down one more. This time, the clutch only allowed me to go down one at first. So, all of a sudden I was entering the corner a gear too high and 5mph too fast, which pushed me a yard wide.

That was all Chili needed to come underneath me. It was then just a case of hanging on because, as he came past, it looked as though he had more tyre left and immediately pulled a bit of a gap on me. At the start of the final lap he had half a second lead, although I still thought I had a chance of winning. My favourite section was down Craner Curves and through the Old Hairpin. I closed up on him there and was with him by Coppice.

As we came down the straight he braked really late, which I knew he would. I didn't even think about making an attempt to pass him because I thought he would mess up his line into the Esses, but he held his line well and then went on the defensive. My last chance to pass was at the Loop and the only thing that cost me the race – and I didn't realise it until I saw the race on video this evening – was that I waited just too long to turn the throttle coming out of the Loop. I almost waited for him to get on the gas before I did. That's the only criticism I'd make of myself throughout the whole weekend. If I'd turned it earlier, I might have 'high-sided', then again I might not. But the fact that I hesitated made the difference between being level with him when we hit the brakes and being a bike's length behind.

Maybe, just maybe, if I'd already won five races this year and was flying, I'd have tried to stick it underneath him at the last corner, where it's so difficult to pass. But there would probably have been contact because he braked late. It would have been just like the time when Loris Capirossi knocked Tetsuya Harada off in the final 250cc Grand Prix of 1998 by not shutting off the gas. So, knowing the track so well and having seen a lot of crashes there, I knew that the risk far outweighed the possible consequences by 100–1 and I settled for second place. I was really pleased with that. Considering what had happened with the bike, I'd ridden bloody well. The old Neil Hodgson would have finished seventh and been quite pleased with himself.

The next three hours was spent doing PR and signing autographs and it was a pleasant three hours. I wouldn't have minded if it had been for 10 hours, now the racing was over. In fact I didn't have my first beer at the track until 8pm and it went straight to my head. All my Burnley friends were down visiting and we went on to the Thistle Hotel where Jamie Whitham's band, The Po Boys, were playing. The weekend's tension had finally gone and the beer went straight to my head – helped by the fact that I was still dehydrated from the races. But it was a nice drunken feeling and I was going for it on the dancefloor. Every so often I had to come out because I was wringing with sweat, but I didn't care for once because I didn't feel on show in front of a load of punters. And the ones that were there all had really nice things to say. After so many trials at the start of the season the sense of relief to have finally succeeded and rewarded the efforts of Darrell, the team and the fans was over-powering. This is what it's all about!

We ended up back at the motorhome, where the Burnley posse was sleeping. All we had to eat were some frozen sausages which we tried to fry. After an hour's frying, they ended up in an uncooked mash at the bottom of the pan, with the motorhome's smoke alarm going off every two minutes. I tried to eat it but realised that I would probably die of food poisoning or a burnt tongue, so I whizzed the remains – along with the pan – into the paddock.

I eventually fell asleep to the sound of one of my friends, who had got hold of Colin's mobile, ringing all his saved numbers. He got through to one woman at four in the morning, asking her why she had stood him up at 10 o'clock. The poor woman didn't have a clue what was happening. And, by that stage, neither did I!

Monday, 28 May 2001

Don't feel very well…

EuroSpeedway Lausitz
– round 7

Wednesday, 6 June 2001

It had been a nice change to leave Donington feeling pretty relieved that my season had been kick-started. All of a sudden, I was only 57 points behind championship leader Troy Bayliss and, with seven rounds to go, my championship challenge had finally been reignited. A successful weekend also refills your 'fuel tank' so, although I was mentally tired, I threw myself into my training for the next five days. Kathryn was away flying and couldn't believe how tired I looked when she returned to the island.

'I think you've been doing too much,' she said.

'I don't think it's that, it's probably just that I'm still recovering from last weekend. It's amazing how much it can take out of you,' I replied.

However, there was very little chance to recharge my batteries. This was the first time a round had been staged at Lausitzring, a brand new £100 million circuit situated in the countryside between Dresden and Berlin. It had therefore been decided to stage a day's official testing on the Wednesday before the race, so that the riders and teams could try to get to know the track.

115

Kathryn was working until Friday night, so James came with me in the motorhome and we had a real laugh. I picked him up at Donington and, after the ferry trip from Dover, everything seemed to be going smoothly, enough until our motorway journey came to an abrupt stop somewhere in Holland. From happily travelling along in the usual three lanes, I was suddenly faced with traffic lights at a t-junction. James was frantically trying to read a map that, in his defence, was very complicated. But we had no idea what to do and I ended up stopping slap-bang in the middle of the busiest intersection imaginable. Luckily it was the middle of the night, so the traffic was not too busy but the horns soon started beeping. Although I knew we were getting lost, I had no other option but to carry on and try to do a U-turn, and believe me, this motorhome is not the easiest thing to turn round. I managed something like a 25-point turn, bringing the traffic in both directions to a halt, which seemed to annoy the Dutch motorists! All I could do was wave at them and smile as if to say 'It's okay, I'm foreign. I'm allowed to do this!'

When we arrived here on Tuesday afternoon, my first impressions of the Eurospeedway circuit, as it's also called, were not good. It might have a massive and spectacular grandstand but this is another tight and twisty track, a bit like Valencia. And the corners are slow, which doesn't make for exciting racing in my book. It seems that whenever new circuits are built nowadays the designers try to squeeze them into the smallest space available. Give me a classic racing layout like Brno, Spa or Assen any day.

The day was split into four one-hour sessions and I was third after the first hour. 'This is going to be all right,' I thought. I improved by two or three tenths of a second in the next session but everyone else went a second quicker, so I dropped down to

11th. The same thing happened in the first session of the afternoon. My times were up by the same margin but the others went another half a second faster, then I was down in 14th, yet I felt like I was breaking the lap record on every lap. I was concerned, to say the least, because we were not making any headway.

Before the final hour I had a debriefing with Stewart and talked him through every corner. He hit the nail on the head straight away. Donington has a lot of long fast corners, where the suspension loads up on the rear and tends to push you wide. We had put a harder spring on so that it wouldn't load so much and I could keep a tighter line, but we arrived in Germany still with that harder setting which was not suited to a track like this with a lot of first and second gear corners. I was losing grip and the bike was also very nervous through the chicane. When we changed things for the final hour I went 1.3 seconds quicker. That was only good enough for ninth, but I was just 0.6 seconds off the pace and 0.2 behind Ruben Xaus in third.

My best decision of the day was to go and eat with the team at their hotel, rather than moping around at the circuit on my own. After dinner they all went to an Irish bar around the corner, at about 10.30pm. Normally, in a race week, I'd try to be getting ready for bed around that time, but all I would have done if I'd gone back would have been to start getting stressed about the races. This was probably a better way of resting and relaxing and the team was in good form.

I paired up with Dave Parkes to take everyone on at pool. Now I'm no slouch at pool, but I'm probably the worst in the whole team. However, we were a perfect double act and managed to stay on for ages – not to mention seven-balling James and Frankie, who really are good. To me, Dave is the backbone of the team. His background is in touring cars, having worked with Andy Rouse, but he has known Darrell for a long time and is very loyal to him. If I were ever to advise anyone with regard to putting a team together, his would be the first name on the list. He takes his work so personally, especially if I break down. Obviously Stewart is the first guy I speak to about the bike when we're in the garage, but Dave is always keen to find out how I'm feeling on a personal level. And he never ever makes a mistake. Something that sums up what I think about him was on the Thursday at Phillip Island. All the preparation had been done and the team were given a day off, but he could not keep away from the track.

'Chill out, Dave. Go and see the penguins or something,' I said to him.

He looked at me with deadly seriousness, and said: 'No, Neil, when I'm racing, I'm racing. I want to make sure that nothing goes wrong here.' You just can't buy those team player qualities. (And you can't buy a wife like his. She's the most attractive older woman I know – really youthful in her outlook and brilliant fun.

Thursday, 7 June 2001

Our usual walk around the track with Stewart and James was more eventful than usual. It was seven o'clock and, as is normally the case, the track was full of people, walking, cycling, jogging and there was even a girl roller-blading round. Then, all of a sudden, two yellow Audis – which looked like safety cars – came screeching around the corner.

'Bloody hell lads, stand back,' I shouted.

The cars tore into the next corner, despite the fact that there was a girl there on her push-bike. 'This is getting stupid,' I thought. Two minutes later and they were back, at exactly the same speed. If this had been at any other track in the world, somebody would have been going mad with them. But they looked semi-official, so maybe nobody dared tell them that what they were doing was dangerous.

We carried on walking until the next long corner, where there were some straw bales at the side of the track. If they had been carrying on at the same speed, the cars were probably about a quarter of a lap away.

'Hey, watch this,' I said to James and Stewart, throwing two huge bales into the middle of the track. When the cars came charging round, they screeched to a stop and one of the guys jumped out of his car. 'Here we go again,' I thought, because every time I come to Germany I end up in trouble.

'You. Come here now!' he yelled. James and Stewart panicked and stopped, but I ignore him and carried on walking.

'Don't listen to him, just carry on walking,' I said.

By now the bloke had got back into his car, drove around the straw bales and had parked next to James and Stewart, so I then felt obliged to walk back.

'You move those straw bales now,' he shouted at James and myself. He was obviously unsure of who had thrown them there.

'Don't do anything, James,' I said, and because I was doing the talking, his attention turned to me.

'Move those bales now.'

'No, I didn't put them there.'

'Yes, you did.'

'No, I didn't.'

This was obviously getting him nowhere fast, so he moved the bales himself, jumped back into the car and sped off. While they were away I decided to tie my shoelaces.

'I've got a feeling I might need to be a bit sharp on my feet,' I said to the lads, who were killing themselves laughing by now.

Ten minutes later and the Germans came back round. The same bloke leapt out of the car again, but now he was ten times more officious.

'I have seen the video and it was you. You are now in big trouble,' he barked.

'Calm down! You can't do anything,' I said, as he pulled out an official's pass. I suppose it was meant to impress me but it still meant nothing as far as I was concerned.

'You come with me in the car now,' he said.

'You're not the police. I'm not going anywhere,' I replied, getting that shaky-leg feeling that starts when there's trouble brewing. I love it when the adrenaline is flowing, though. It reminded me of school, when I was always fighting – although I always got battered. In the first couple of years at secondary school I was pretty tough but I didn't grow much after that. So when the others grew into men, and I stayed just as cheeky, I got some proper hidings. I hate fighting now and the last thing I want at the end of a night is to be rolling round in the gutter with some idiot who is trying to smash a glass in your face. I fully expected this guy to grab me and, if he didn't let go when I told him to, I would probably have to punch him.

'You pack your bags now,' he shouted, getting more and more frustrated. I couldn't stop myself from laughing loudly in his face, which really bugged him and he stormed off back to the car again. When we returned to the garage, their cars were outside the organizers' office so I told Colin what had happened because I was sure we'd not heard the last of it.

Friday, 8 June 2001

The last thing you want, when you are trying to learn a new circuit, is rain. And, of course, it rained this morning. We'd heard that a championship race had been cancelled the previous week because the track was too dangerous and slippery when wet. It's because they've used an unusual kind of tarmac, which does not allow the water to 'sit down' but leaves it standing on the surface.

Colin decided that we should sit out the first 20 minutes and let some of the others find out just how bad the track was. That way, we were not going to find out the hard way by sliding down the track and breaking our wrists. When it finally seemed that everyone was coping okay, I went out and just rode round for a few laps to build up my confidence. I was getting faster, but ended the session down in 15th, 3.5 seconds behind Troy Bayliss, but that was just down to the fact that I'd had a lot less track time than the others in those conditions. There was a nagging doubt, though, that if it was wet on race day, I might be at a slight disadvantage because we had missed those few extra vital minutes. But I'd had long enough out there to realise that the gearing and set-up were wrong for wet conditions, which is unusual for me because I normally keep the same set-up for wet and dry conditions. At least we knew in what direction we were heading should it carry on raining.

The track was starting to dry for the afternoon qualifying session and a lot of the riders went out on intermediates. I went round to the garage of the Motorola Supersport team to ask Vito Guareschi and his team-mate Dean Thomas, what they had used for their practice session which had just ended. They both advised slicks and, although it was still a bit damp, I soon had it confirmed that there was enough grip when Corser came flying past me straight away. That gave me enough confidence to get my head down and do six or seven quite fast laps on a narrow drying line. Then it started to drizzle and I went straight back to the pits, anticipating to be up there with the leaders, but not expecting to be fastest with a time of 1:43.018. It's a nice feeling to have read the conditions right. James had started on intermediates and, when he did decide to change to slicks, didn't know how fast to push it and finished the session in 20th. It rained hard for 30 minutes but then I went out to do another six or seven laps to test the new lower gearing, which felt a lot better and provided far more grip.

Saturday, 8 June 2001

This morning's final qualifying was a disaster. I've now used Japanese Dunlops in the last four meetings and we tested them here on Wednesday. As usual, they'd given us consistent performance after about five laps. We knew then that we had a trump card up our sleeves in that we'd already decided what race tyre we were going to use, but we only had enough tyres to use for the Superpole warm-up session in the afternoon. I was back on English Dunlops for most of the morning qualifying before sticking a Japanese tyre in towards the end for a few fast laps and then a qualifier at the death to finish fourth, 0.32 seconds behind Corser. However, on race tyres, I was second fastest behind Edwards.

The plan, therefore, for the afternoon was to try and demoralize everyone else by stringing about 16 or 17 laps together in the 1:40s. After five laps I was still in the low 41s. And after eight laps I was in the high 41s, and by lap 11, I'd slipped into the 42s. This was not going to plan. The back end was sliding everywhere on closed throttle and, when I came in after 15 laps, the tyre had completely torn. This wasn't worn, it was shredded. Everybody stood around, scratching their heads because we were back to square one with 30 minutes of practice left, and I was getting pretty stressed.

Colin suggested that I try to do as many laps as possible on the 747 English tyre again but it didn't feel good and once again, I was in the low 42s. We'd finished qualifying not knowing whether the English tyre would last the race distance, and knowing that our supposed trump card of the Japanese tyre certainly wouldn't. I was not doing a good job in disguising my panic.

'Look! Stop worrying about everything. Your job today is to finish this session and then focus on Superpole,' said Colin, sternly.

'But surely we need to try a different set-up?' I asked, my mind racing.

'Forget about the set-up, we'll talk about that after Superpole,' Colin assured me.

The dramas had made me more nervous than usual for Superpole. So it was 'Hello' to the old Neil Hodgson when the first few riders went out and produced good times in Superpole.

'Well, I'm going to qualify on the third or fourth row here. There's no doubt about that,' I thought. I had totally been taken over by negative thoughts.

When I went out for my lap I got the first corner all wrong and that was probably the best thing that could have happened. It clicked me into focus and I went on to put a really hard lap together. The rest of the first section was okay and the same went for the middle section. But, through braking too late into the first gear hairpin, the back end came round way too much, and I couldn't turn into the corner properly. All I could do was keep braking and, as soon as the bike came slightly back into line, I threw the bike back onto my knee and got onto the power. You can do that on a qualifier and especially on the condom-soft tyre that I was using for this non-abrasive circuit. It was a bit risky but it was a good piece of riding, even if I say so myself. It probably saved me a tenth of a second, which was going to make a difference here and, when I took the final corner as aggressively as I had done all week, I knew my time was good. However, Bayliss and Corser were still to go, so I had to wait to find out whether I was on pole, although I knew I'd done well enough to put on a show for the crowd. For the second consecutive meeting, though, my celebration lap did not quite go to plan as I slid too far into one corner, realised I wasn't going to make it and had to run off down a slip-road and miss out a quarter of the lap.

From the panic of a few minutes earlier, I was feeling on top of the world. That just about lasted until the end of the press conferences. If anything, I'd put more pressure on myself, knowing that we didn't have a race tyre, so the elation flicked straight back to misery, and the gremlins were back. 'This is going to be the old Neil Hodgson: Qualifies well and rides round in 20th', I thought to myself.

After a shower I had a meeting with Stewart and John Higgins – Higgy – the Dunlop tyre technician. The relationship between rider and tyre man is another very important part of the overall team package. I've worked with Higgy for a couple of years and he was a big factor in me winning the British title last year. So I was delighted when I discovered that he'd be coming with us to World Superbikes. He's pretty reserved, and a man who doesn't waste his words. But that's a good type of person to have around the garage. There's nothing worse than someone who comes in shouting their mouth off when I'm trying to work. I've nothing but respect for Higgy's opinion and I can read him like a book now. He might say 'This tyre should be okay' and I will know that he's not sure. Similarly when he says 'This will be okay', I know that it will be okay.

So when Higgy said 'Basically, we're in the shit', I knew that we were well and truly in the shit.

'Corser is going to run the soft Japanese that you've tried. And you know what that's going to do. Bostrom is going with the English tyre that you've sort of tried, but I don't think that it is going to last. Or there's another English tyre that's slightly harder than the one that Bostrom's going to use, but nobody has tried it before and you'd be the only rider on it. If you're happy with it, I'd advise you to go with that one,' he said.

I'd have slept on the decision, if I'd been able to get to sleep!

Sunday, 9 June 2001

We used the new tyre for warm-up and it didn't look too bad after 10 laps, although it was starting to mark up and grain. But I was third fastest behind Edwards and Okada, the two Castrol Honda men on Michelin tyres.

'It might be starting to tear,' said Higgy. 'But the track temperature is rising, so that's only going to help. I'm 90 per cent sure that it's going to stay clean.'

There was no real choice to make, and I actually felt pretty smug, thinking that I had a pretty good tyre up my sleeve. I knew that the likes of Corser and Chili were definitely going to tear, so I had no doubt that I was going to be the top Dunlop rider.

'You might do the first few laps a bit slower than the riders on the Japanese tyre, which has more side grip. If you can stay with them early on, you know that after 10 laps they're going to come back to you and you're going to get them,' added Higgy.

That's not how it worked out.

I had a decent start and tucked in behind the leader, Colin Edwards. Five or six laps into the race I was all over him. 'This is much easier than expected. This was supposed to be the hard part of the race,' I thought. I considered passing him on a couple of occasions but his bike has a bit more acceleration than mine and, while I came out of a couple of corners right up his tail-pipe, he would immediately pull three or four metres. I'm good enough on the brakes to pull that distance back, but you need to make up another three or four metres to actually make a pass.

I was happy to sit behind, knowing that he was doing all the work, then, on lap nine, he suddenly disappeared. He'd pulled a second on me within two or three corners. I'd had a couple of slight slides, but didn't think I'd done that much wrong, and he continued to pull away throughout the lap. I quickly realised that I'd lost all side grip and could no longer carry any corner speed. 'Maybe that's just a sharp drop-off and it'll stay the same until the end of the race,' I thought and hoped.

No such luck! From then on the tyre got progressively worse, to the extent that I was nearly four seconds a lap slower than the leaders at the end of the race. By then, Bayliss, Okada, Corser, Chili, Lavilla and Laconi had all passed me, I was down in eighth place and nearly falling off in every corner.

It was, without doubt, the worst tyre I've ever had in my career. In the space of one lap it had gone from being awesome to nearly unrideable. Talk about coming back down to earth with a bump after Donington. I was totally demoralized because I was riding so well and I wanted to erect a big sign that told everyone just how bad the tyre had been. I know the other riders had had problems, but nowhere near as bad as mine.

Higgy came straight up to me to apologise. 'We made a mistake and I'm really sorry,' he said.

'Don't worry about it. At the end of the day it was my decision to go with it,' I said. There was no point going off on one. The guy takes his job totally seriously, so there was nothing to be gained from making him feel any worse than he did already.

However, we still had to come up with a plan for the second

race. We decided to use the Japanese tyre so that at least we knew I'd be in the same boat as Corser and Chili. I still felt that I was riding well enough to beat them – on a level playing field.

I knew I could do better than that on a wet playing field, so I was really chuffed when it started to rain between races.

'Yep, that'll do for me,' I thought, knowing that if the track was just slightly damp I didn't have to worry about tyre choice. The only thing I was now a bit paranoid about was starting a wet race in pole, because you move directly onto a thick white line and can lose all drive on the slippery paint. From the second row, you have a chance to gather some momentum before you hit the start-finish line. Stewart told me to do a small burn-out when I got back to the line after the warm-up lap. I'd never done this before but the theory is to clear the water from directly under the tyre and to get some temperature in the middle of the tread. It worked a treat and I led into the first corner.

But the first lap felt so slow, as if I was riding round on eggshells. I was amazed to find out that Bayliss and I had pulled clear of the rest. Troy passed me at the start-finish line at the end of the first lap and started to set a very good pace. So it was just a case of trying to stay with him at that stage. I didn't know what was happening behind me because I couldn't look at my board properly and gauge my braking point at the same time, especially in the wet when you brake a lot sooner. It was only when the visibility improved marginally later on that I noticed I was +20 on third place. 'That can't be right, it must be +2,' I thought and had a look over my shoulder at the first opportunity to check.

I then knew that it was a straight fight between Bayliss and myself, with 10 laps to go. Or at least it was a straight fight until my clutch lever went floppy again, just as it had at Donington. This is even more of a handicap in the wet, as you need all the control you can get. I knew that I wasn't going to win the race. I was losing three-quarters of a second a lap on Bayliss and was realistically concentrating on finishing in second.

He didn't manage to pull any further away than three seconds, and I was surprised by how much control I still had left, despite the clutch. Maybe his tyres were softer than mine and were starting to drop off. With five laps remaining, the tension came back in the clutch. Don't ask me why it happens, it just does! And it was a great feeling because I could then brake later and feed the clutch out into the corners.

I started to reel Troy in and at that stage, I was confident I'd be able to do him. He was better through the tight chicane third corner, where his bike had a horsepower advantage on mine, and where he pulled away slightly on each lap. So, for the last lap, I knew I had to minimise this distance.

Braking into the corner after the chicane, the gap was down to a second but the next sections were my best. I closed right up and was immediately behind him for the long right hander, where again his bike was so much faster. Even though I was in his slipstream out of the corner, he accelerated away down the next straight and now there were only three corners remaining.

There was still only a narrow dry racing line for the next two corners and the only way I'd have been able to overtake was on the inside on the wetter line. That would definitely have resulted in me crashing – or us both crashing! So the only thing I could do, until the last corner where there was only one line, was to stay right behind him and hope for a mistake.

It came. Troy had a big slide but, as a result of that, he had closed off the throttle. However, my rear was spinning and because I was hard on the gas, trying to capitalize, he was able to get the drive away down the straight to win by 0.229 of a second.

This was a result that I'd needed. I'd expected to be

challenging in both races and was on a major downer after the first race. After winning at Donington, I felt that I needed to prove myself outside England. This second place, along with pole position, had gone some way towards doing that, and the most important thing was that I knew I was now riding well. It also meant that I'd pulled the points gap to Corser, in third place, back to 31 and I was only 12 behind Chili on fourth. If I could finish third in the championship in my first year back, and after the start that I've suffered with a new team on a year-old bike, it would feel like a win.

I've also decided to make the most of the good times when they come along, because you can be sure that there'll be more bad times round the corner. We went back to the Irish bar near the team hotel and I got ratted. Coming out onto the street at 3am it seemed like a good idea to 'borrow' a scruffy old push-bike which was parked nearby. Maybe I was hoping that it belonged to the official from Thursday night. But, after mucking around on it for a while, I decided to take it back – if only for a bit of karma!

Misano – round 8

Thursday, 21 June 2001

We set off from a deserted Lausitzring paddock at lunchtime, with a bit of a hangover. There was no point driving back to the Isle of Man as we'd have had a maximum of three days there before setting off again for Italy. I knew there was a nice campsite near Misano where we could stay for a week's holiday. I had camped there in 1993, when I was riding a 125cc in the Italian Grand Prix, along with Dave Jefferies and two of my heroes at the time, Kevin Schwantz and Niall Mackenzie.

Schwantz invited me into his motorhome at one point, and it was like nothing I'd ever seen before – absolutely massive. And I was so overawed that I couldn't help myself firing about a thousand questions at him inside a minute.

What's it like on a 500cc? What do you do for training? What do you eat? Do you do motocross…?' I rabbited.

'Jeez man, you're keen,' he said. Dave still reminds me of how embarrassing I was.

Anyway, I drove for around nine hours until we reached the Dolomites near Lake Garda and pulled in at some services. Having found a parking spot, Kathryn noticed that we were surrounded by gypsies. There was no way we would have survived the night in a motorhome filled with attractive gadgets, so we decided to drive on to the next services.

'But they'll know what you're doing,' Kathryn said, when we set off. 'They'll just come and find us at the next place,' she added, making me totally paranoid. So we skipped that one and drove to the following one after that. There were no parking places there, though, so off we went again to the next services and finally settled down for the night to nurse my hangover.

It was only another three hours to the campsite the next day and we arrived to find that the electrics in the motorhome wouldn't work. Chris, the guy driving Corser's motorhome around, was already there and tried to help out, along with Corser's personal fitness trainer, 'KO'. All the while that Chris was on the phone back to Travelworld – he had a lot more experience of these things so there was no point me talking to them – I was developing a proper three-year-old sulk. I know when it's happening, but I still can't see beyond the end of my nose. It's a weird feeling because I'm saying to myself 'Come on, you're acting like an idiot' but can't seem to do anything about it.

'Come on, we'll go for a walk to calm you down,' Kathryn suggested.

'No, I don't want to,' I replied.

'So what are you going to do – sit here and sulk?' she asked.

'Yep. I'm selling this thing. And I'm getting a flight back to England, because I'm not sitting in this thing for a week without electricity,' I ranted.

'Just think about everyone else here,' reasoned Kathryn. 'They're all staying in tents.'

'Yeah, but I paid tens of thousands of pounds for this thing while they paid £3 for a tent,' I argued.

Chris couldn't believe that I wasn't carrying any tools with the motorhome.

'Look, Chris, I had a £300 car at home without any tools and that never broke down. So I didn't really expect this to be breaking down all the time,' I moaned.

The standing joke is now for them to bring little bits and pieces round, the most recent being a double-ended screwdriver, so that I have a very basic tool kit. Chris eventually discovered that the problem was the inverter and we needed a new battery charger. It was not easy getting the local electrical shop in Riccione to know what the hell we were talking about.

When we were finally sorted out we had a fantastic week on the campsite. There were a few other riders hanging around because Honda, Ducati and Aprilia were all testing there that week. The same teams also had a test here last month for two days, on top of this week's two-day session, so they effectively have had a four-day start on us going into this round. It was never even an issue that we would be able to test here. This has nothing to do with funding, it's down to the amount of time that our one engine-builder, Stewart, has available. And since Germany he has worked flat-out every day from seven in the morning until ten at night. That's just to get the engines ready for here and Laguna, because the bikes are crated up after this weekend ready for the trip to America. It would have been impossible for him to prepare engines for a two-day test as well as this round. It's not as though we could get someone else in to help him out, because there's nobody else good enough. So, because a test was never on the cards, there was no suggestion that I was pissed off about it.

It has been a good opportunity for getting to know people like Colin Edwards. Until this week I have really only formed an impression of him through what I've read in papers and magazines. I probably thought 'He's not a bad person, but not my kind of person.' But the press does not provide you with a true picture and I guess I was a little bit jealous, because he is roughly the same age and has had more success. Now I know that he's bob on and the kind of bloke I could spend more time with, although he did beat me at tennis!

Edwards is massively into rock-climbing after being introduced to it by Ben Bostrom. In fact Bostrom spent a night before the Phillip Island round stranded on a ledge in freezing temperatures when a climb in the Blue Mountains went wrong. Colin took a group of us, including Marty Craggill, Chris, KO, Taya, one of the Ducati hospitality hostesses, and her boyfriend Nigel Arnold, and he was a really good teacher – very patient with everybody. But, even though I'm not scared of heights and knew that I could only drop so far because I was clipped on, it didn't stop my breathing being affected through anxiety. I made it to the top, though, and was really impressed when Kathryn got up there on her second attempt, which is more than Craggill did!

Marty is another top bloke, but someone I might only have said 'hello' to in the past. We went for a mountain bike ride to San Marino, which is a 50 miles round trip and uphill all the way there. He was on a proper racing bike, while I was on a large tank of a thing with a big, numb plastic seat, so I was knackered when we got there after a couple of hours, although San Marino is worth the effort.

Friday, 22 June 2001

The fact that we were playing catch-up showed immediately as I was about a second off the early pace on race tyres with a time of 1:37.778 compared to 1:36.640 from Edwards. But this is a track at which you need to find your feet. The surface is terrible – old and bumpy – and, coming from a brand new circuit like Lausitzring, it was a shock to the system. It takes some time for your brain to register the rough surface in front of you, with repairs, wallows and cracks. All the time you have to be telling yourself 'I don't want to be giving it a big handful over there.' So even just those recent couple of days testing would have stood me in better stead.

In the afternoon I fell into the trap of trying too many different things at once. We experimented with a slightly different tyre, different gearing, suspension, harder fork springs and a stiffer rear shock. It was too much to take in all at once and I couldn't see the wood for the trees. So instead of riding the bike hard, I was concentrating too much on the response of the bike. I'm as guilty as anybody, because I come into the garage saying 'We need to do this, we need to try that.' But the team also realised they were at fault for not sticking to the golden rule of changing one thing at a time.

However, I did manage to do 20 laps on a rear tyre, which looked okay. The front tyre was tending to fold under, though. I was using the softest construction plus the softest rubber and it couldn't quite cope with these hot temperatures. I tried a harder front but it wasn't as good so I'll have to accept that the front will give good grip, but might move around a bit. Again I finished the session in ninth, 1.2 seconds behind Bayliss, but with a couple of guys, Mauro Sanchini and Steve Martin in front of me, that shouldn't really have been happening. So I wasn't in the best frame of mind.

I took Kathryn for a scooter lesson on the track in the evening and, once more, she took to it really well and was moving smoothly between cones. But the problem was she couldn't pull the thing back onto the stand when she got off, so she's not ready to start racing me, or even go on the roads yet!

Saturday, 23 June 2001

It was too hot last night. There's the option of sleeping with the air conditioning on, of course, but that's too noisy and also stops me from sleeping. To cap it all, it was also really windy and, having left the awning up, it felt like the motorhome was going to take off. However, I didn't fancy the thought of having to wake Kathryn up in the middle of the night to help me take it down – because I need the instruction book to do it on my own.

We'd made a couple of changes to the bike overnight – slightly lower gearing and also adding some oil to the forks, which hardens them up at the lower end. This was because we were putting a bit too much pressure on the tyres at the bottom of the stroke. As with most of Stewart's ideas, it worked straight away. It's great that he doesn't expect me to come up with these solutions. You do hear about riders who come back into the garage and tell their technicians 'I want two clicks here or three clicks there'. All the top engineers that I've spoken to, however, say they prefer working with a rider like me who will just tell them when the bike is chattering at the front or where it is running wide at corners. That way they can translate those messages into actual changes without reinventing the wheel, and all I have to do is say 'Better or worse'.

I managed to improve my time on race rubber, the softest Japanese tyre available, by half a second and, while I was making progress, it seemed that the other riders had hit a brick wall. On qualifying tyres I was nearly 1.5 seconds quicker than yesterday, so I felt a bit more relaxed on the bike. Plus I hadn't spent the session fretting about problems and, as a result, had felt less tense and tired.

We were told between sessions that some of the other Dunlop riders had tried a slightly smaller rear wheel rim width – 6 inches compared to the 6.25 that I'd been using – and had found it better. The smaller size changes the profile of the tyre. With Japanese tyres having better side grip than drive grip, they spin when you pick the bike up coming out of corners. If you flatten the tyre out with a larger rim, there's more of a contact patch for improved drive. But, going the other way to a smaller rim, as in this case, obviously does the opposite, and, because there is a lot of long horseshoe corners at Misano, you need as much side grip as possible.

I wanted to do as many laps as I could on race set-up in the afternoon and managed to put in 15 hard laps before dropping off a bit for the final five or six. That's because I hit a bit of traffic and didn't want to do anything silly at that late stage. Then the final few minutes were freed up to do a few one lap wonders in preparation for Superpole.

While I'm still anxious before my lap, after my recent success I've lost my early season nerves and am now quite relaxed about it. It also helps that the Dunlop qualifying tyre is better than the Michelin. A perfect lap around here is to be smooth through the first section, which is a bit like Donington, and then aggressive on the final section, which is more like Lausitzring. I was actually thinking about other things going into the first couple of corners – not what I was having for my tea, but just telling myself to concentrate as I had felt slow going into the final corner of my warm-up lap. And when I wasn't hard enough on the throttle into the first corner, I was urging myself to concentrate even harder for the second corner. In fact, I was concentrating so hard on making myself concentrate that I wasn't actually concentrating – if you see what I mean!

Anyway, I snapped out of it and wasn't even aware of a big slide halfway round which they kept repeating on the television pictures. I did slide it into the final bend, but that was intentional. It must have worked because I was fastest, with five riders remaining. Colin Edwards, however, was the closest with a time of 1:35.532, compared to my time of 1:35.235 and I had another pole position.

That's a great feeling, but probably not the most important consideration on a Saturday evening. At least here, compared to Germany, I can go to bed tonight in the knowledge that I've got a tyre that will last the race. It will be sliding around for the last five laps, but that will be the same for everyone.

Another important development during today was that Darrell and Colin had a meeting with Ducati's top dogs to discuss what would be available to us for next season, providing we can pull in some sponsorship and Darrell decides to run the team again. It's still quite early on in the season but by the time Laguna is out of the way and certainly after Brands, I'll be paying that issue a lot more attention. The way I feel at the moment is that I'd be 100 per cent happy to stay with this team because we have learned a lot and I am riding better than at the start of the season.

What I do want, though, is to be on the latest bike. Whenever I have been following Troy Bayliss's Ducati round, he gains a lot coming out of the corners. I know that if I were on that bike, I'd be able to do the same. It might not mean much per lap, but two tenths can make all the difference. The early indications, though, are that we'd still be running one-year old bikes from Ducati. So that means I still have to keep every option open.

My priority is to be with the right team but money is also an issue because I have a short career and I want to earn as much as I possibly can. If I finish third in the world championship, I'll want to be paid my market worth. Having said that, I wouldn't jeopardise the chance of winning the world championship just go somewhere else for more money. On the right bike, I feel that my best chance of doing that would be to stay with GSE Racing, because, so far, I think we've been doing a really good job.

The only problem is this business of sponsorship. I'm sure everyone is pointing the finger at my manager Roger Burnett, who is trying to find a backer for us. But it isn't easy and I know that Roger has a lot of professional people working for him who are all trying their hardest. He actually has a number of roles, as his company, RBP, also handles the publicity for the team, while Roger works as a commentator for the BBC. This weekend, though, he has not had the same broadcasting workload and has been out there for every session, giving me words of valuable advice. For instance, he'll tell me that Bayliss might be using fifth gear through the last corner, while I'm using fourth. And, if Bayliss is quicker there, then it's a great help to know those things. It's impossible to quantify it, but he's saved me a lot of time over the years.

Sunday, 24 June 2001

I had a new engine in my number one bike for warm-up because the other one had done 800kms and the most you normally get is 1,000 maximum. It felt pretty good until, coming out of one corner, the bike cut-out, picked up immediately and then cutout again. The dashboard readings had gone off, so I was sure that it wasn't anything too serious, probably just an electrical fault. Even so, Colin decided not to gamble when it was discovered that the alternator was faulty, and told me to start the first race on my second bike.

'We're not 100 per cent sure it's fixed,' he said. 'So it's best not to take any chances.'

The second bike should have been identical in set-up and performance and, while I could understand the thinking behind the decision, I still felt it was strange as my number one bike definitely felt faster. The engine actually lacked a bit of punch and I was losing ten yards on all the factory riders going down the straight and, no matter how good a rider you are, you're fighting a losing battle in that situation. It might be okay for riders who think that doing their job is to ride round in eighth place, but I'm trying to do a lot more than that.

My start was, at best, average and I had dropped to fourth or fifth going into the first corner and was fourth by the end of the first lap. Then Bayliss came past on the next lap and I was down to sixth when Gregorio Lavilla overtook me on the sixth lap. I immediately realised that I'd been caught out big-style by not really racing anyone during qualifying. I'd been happy to ride round on my own, judging my own braking points. But, in the race, I realised that I hadn't been braking late enough in practice – probably by about five or six yards. Instead, I was trying to ride smoothly by braking, letting the brake off and carrying as much corner speed as possible. I needed to be braking at the last minute and, instead of worrying about corner speed, getting out of the corner as quickly as possible. However, because of the way the bike was set-up, I couldn't brake any later as the front forks were already bottoming. If you continue to brake at that point it just pushes the tyre too much and the bike can hop and run wide.

So, all things considered, I was up against it. I briefly regained fifth when I overtook Corser on the 12th lap but then dropped back to seventh when Regis Laconi came through before retiring on lap 17. That left a three-way dice for fifth place with Yanagawa and Corser. I was confident of being able to make a move on Yanagawa in front of me and I was determined to stay in front of Corser in order to pull some points back on him in the championship standings.

With three or four corners to go, at one of the horseshoes, a rider came clattering into my leg and hip, leaving rubber on my leathers. At first, I had no idea who it was and was sure that they were going to crash, because I had leaned on them and pushed myself wide in order to stay on my bike. But then Corser came underneath me and I realised that it must have been him whom I'd touched. He was so lucky to stay on. I was devastated because he had gained half a second on me when I'd been forced wide.

Then, amazingly, he made a brave old move on Yanagawa going into the last corner and pushed them both wide. That allowed me to get the slingshot and pass Corser going over the line, beating him by three thousandths of a second, while Yanagawa hung on for fifth. For a moment it felt like winning the race because I'd earned my corn by riding as hard as I could with the engine under-performing and the set-up all wrong.

'That's the toughest sixth place I've ever had. Winning at Donington was a piece of cake compared to that,' I told Kathryn.

There were clearly some changes to be made for the second race. For starters, I was back on the number one bike although it was still a case of 'We hope' rather than 'We're sure' the alternator has been fixed. We also decided to go to the larger rim width, as my drive grip had been appalling in the first race. Bostrom had used the 6.25 and he'd fared pretty well in giving Bayliss a good run for his money.

I found myself behind Edwards again at the start and didn't want him to hold me up like he had done in the first race, so I dived underneath him at one of the fast kinks. That was quite a scary move, but the changes had obviously been for the better. I was so concerned with braking later that I'd not paid so much attention to my pitboard and, while I knew someone was right up behind me, I had no idea who it was until after about 10 laps. I was also sliding a lot more into the corners and even using my back brake into the last corner, more to position myself on the track correctly than for any other reason. Whether or not I use the back brake depends on the circuit. I might use it here a couple of times a lap, never touch it on other tracks like Lausitzring and then use it on 50 per cent of the corners at Brands Hatch. It's just a 'feel' thing.

When Bostrom came past me with over half of the race remaining, the idea was just to stick with him. That was easier said than done because – on a factory bike – he was constantly pulling away, even if only slightly. He would have been feeling brilliant to see that gap slowly increasing. I wanted to try and make him panic by matching him for a couple of laps. At least I knew that second place was in the bag and a podium finish would make up for the disappointment of the first race.

With four laps to go the back wheel was sliding pretty violently. 'I just hope this tyre is going to be okay,' I thought. With two and a half laps to go, I knew it wasn't! There was an almighty bang, like a bomb going off, on the fastest point of the fast kink. And I knew exactly what had happened.

'Do I carry on or do I stop?' was my immediate thought. 'I might still be able to get some points but it might be dangerous with the tyre in this state,' I was worried, because I couldn't quite see just how big a piece of rubber was missing. I'd have been really fed up if I'd got back to the garage and there was just a small chunk missing, especially if I could have limped round to pick up two or three points. Those points might make the difference between a couple of places at the end of the year. But, for all I knew, I could have been riding on the rim if it had been a puncture and not just a blow-out.

I just tried to nurse it round for a couple of laps and ended up in 16th, one place out of the points. I was told after the race that there were Italian men in the crowd in tears, realising how hard I'd tried. And believe me that there's no pun intended when I say that I felt totally deflated.

In hindsight, it was probably dangerous to have continued.

The tyre had totally delaminated and a strip could easily have locked in the swinging arm, throwing me off the bike. It wasn't any comfort that I wasn't the only Dunlop rider to have suffered problems during the race, with Corser and Yanagawa also struggling. I don't know what state their tyres were in, but I'm pretty certain they were not as bad as mine were. The one guy who didn't have any problems was Bostrom, who won pretty comfortably ahead of Bayliss. He was telling people after the race that he could see I was working my rear tyre hard early on the race and half-expected me to have problems.

I can't help thinking that if we'd been able to test here, we might have known more about how various tyres would perform. The whole team had worked their butts off trying to make sure everything was ready for the race, and I'd tried to do as many laps as possible on race tyres to make sure that another Germany didn't happen. I felt as though I'd done my bit to the best of my ability, however, I feel let down, and I'm sure the team feels the same. That's not to say I'm pointing the finger at Dunlop. I have raced for 11 seasons and used Dunlop for eight of them and nothing like this has happened before, but that doesn't stop them feeling embarrassed and dejected too.

If I did have any lingering hopes of the championship coming to Italy, they have been shredded here. And it's now looking like Troy Bayliss has the title in the bag. I know that he likes the next two tracks – Laguna and Brands – and, although he rides loose and on the edge, he is so consistent. I can't see him throwing it away because he has won championships before. I did actually learn a lot from him in 1999 and, looking towards next year, I've learnt things from his attacking nature this year, and I would rather he won it than anyone else. He was my team-mate just two years ago, so I know him, like him and can relate to him as human being. He does not think he is a God and I don't think he is a God. That's not meant to sound disrespectful, but I know that I'm as good a rider as he is. So if Troy Bayliss can be a world champion, then so can Neil Hodgson.

As far as the rest of this year is concerned for me, I've had a slight setback here and there's no way I'm going to try any less for the remaining rounds. Third place is still in my sights and if I get that I'll be really happy. All I need to do is to try and make the podium at every race meeting. That was my aim on my return to the world championships – to be battling for the lead on television – and we're now approaching something like that. It might seem odd saying that after just finishing sixth and sixteenth, but I'll be going to Laguna full of confidence. All along I knew that if I had problems at the start of the year, I wasn't sure how I would cope mentally. I did have those problems, and I'm really pleased with the way I've coped. It's been a mountain to climb and it has been down to nobody else but me. Now I'm comfortable with competing against and beating people like Edwards and Corser, who I might have put on a slight pedestal in the past, and being in the top three riders in the world.

Laguna Seca – round 9

Monday, 25 June

All I wanted to do last night was to leave the Misano as quickly as possible. We had an 18-hour journey back to England ahead of us and the sooner we left, the sooner we arrived home. Plus, I wasn't exactly in the mood for polite chit-chat after the day's events. I'd already been told that the roads were always bad on Sunday night because all the Italians are returning from the coast to Milan after the weekend, on top of 60,000 people trying to get away from the circuit. A few people had been brave and risked it, but called me to say that there was no point bothering, so we decided to stay at the circuit on Sunday and my plan was to have an early night and set off at 4am.

I hung around Troy Corser's motorhome for a while, trying to be polite but becoming more and more grumpy and didn't even bother having a beer before sneaking off to bed at 11. Kathryn, however, stayed up with Darrell's wife, Michelle, and Kim, Troy Bayliss's wife (although she told me six times not to refer to her as Troy Bayliss's wife!) I expected Kathryn to be back in another hour, but it was probably about 1.30am when she crept in. I say

144

My best start of the year, going into the first corner in the first Laguna race.

Last-minute advice from Stewart on the grid at Laguna. He's the best guy I've ever worked with.

Negotiating the notorious Corkscrew.

You really do feel the heat when you stop racing, especially here in the US.

The old champagne in the face trick ... the only way to stop Bostrom.

ROUND 10: BRANDS HATCH

Colin Wright, the GSE Racing team manager, plots our strategy.

Leading the first race at Brands before it was stopped due to a bad crash.

Roger Burnett is the only other person allowed to kiss Kathryn, a reward for being a fantastic manager over the last 10 years.

Celebrating another 2nd place at Brands with a wheelie.

EUROPEAN ROUND
BRANDS HATCH
27,28,29 JULY 2001

I struggle to come to terms with 2nd place, after Ben Bostrom won the race. Troy Bayliss was on the verge of collapsing due to dehydration.

About to hurl my leathers into the crowd, revealing my Union Jack boxers.

The support at Brands Hatch was the best I've ever experienced.

ROUND 11: OSCHERLEBEN

BBC presenter Suzie
Perry talks to me about
the England football
game before the race at
Oscherleben.

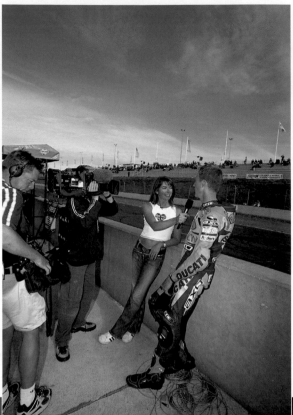

One of the lowest points
of the season came after
the races in Germany.

I was fined £100 for
speeding in the pit-lane
at Assen.

In full flow at Assen.
It was good to come
back strong after the
disappointments of the
previous round.

ROUND 13: IMOLA

Deep in thought preparing
for a Superpole lap at Imola.

I was inconsolable after the
final round.

Baz and Dave fuelling the bikes up for the next race.

Some advice from my ex-team mate and now Vogue model Carl Fogarty! Check out the chin …

… I do next year!

The legendary Halifax mob in action.

Kathryn and I at the top of Table Mountain after my proposal of marriage. Our faces say it all.

On holiday with Darrell in the South of France.

Kathryn, the backbone of all my efforts, looking beautiful as always.

Colin Edwards fixing my safety harness before a climb in San Marino. I think I had other intentions!

Me with the 'Kneel' Hodgson posse at Brands Hatch.

My lucky mascots Flat Eric and Junior try and get in on the act in the motorhome.

crept in, but a brass band could not have made more noise. I was awake, but I pretended to stay asleep.

I woke up at 3.30am before my alarm rang and decided to set off there and then. I let the jacks up, sat in the driver's seat and then shouted back to Kathryn, who was still asleep:

'Right, we're on our way, I need you to read the map.'

'Neil, all the colours on the map are blurring into one,' groaned Kathryn after a few hundred yards, and off she dashed to the toilet to be sick.

I have to stress at this point that this is not a regular occurrence. In fact it's probably because we normally drink so little that we both suffer really bad hangovers. Perhaps we try too hard to keep up with people who are a lot more used to handling their alcohol. Normally, I would have shouted, but I kept my mouth shut and decided to sulk instead, keeping my head down and driving for eight hours until it was time for lunch in central France. I needed a sleep before driving any further and, after nodding off for no more than a few minutes, drove for another three hours before the brake air pressure alarm started to go off.

'I cannot believe this. Not again,' I moaned.

I called Simon at Travelword and could tell straight away from the tone of his voice that it was serious.

'Your brakes are going to lock on if you don't pull over at the next services,' he warned. 'You're going to have to call for some assistance.'

'I can't even begin to try and get my brain around this,' I said to Kathryn, as I started on my next sulk. 'Why me? You speak a bit of French, you are going to have to sort this out because I can't even be bothered to try.'

After she called the breakdown people, a man arrived within half an hour, which was at least a pleasant surprise. However, he just took one look and shook his head, realising this was not just the normal flat tyre that he was used to.

'I must call someone else. They are here in forty minutes,' he said.

Three hours and forty minutes later, a bloke who did not speak a word of English turned up. I tried to start the engine, to show him the problem but then the bloody thing wouldn't start, so he presumed he'd been called to fix that. But, when he sussed out the problem, he went under the motorhome and came out with an odd-looking part.

'Kaput!' he said and I was already preparing to rent a house out for the week. But he was, amazingly, able to fix the problem, which was caused by a stone flicking up and smashing the air pressure release valve. It was a million to one chance of a thing – a bit like your tyre blowing up with two laps to go!

After another eight hours flat out, we made the 11.30pm ferry to Dover. Instead of going up on deck, as you're supposed to, I almost ran to the back of the motorhome, set the alarm for 90 minutes time, and dived on the bed.

The next thing I knew was that Kathryn was shouting:

'Quick, everyone has set off. We're holding everyone up.'

I'd slept through the alarm and didn't know what my name was, never mind which country we were in. That had been the first time I had had any proper sleep for about three nights. A crowd was building up outside the motorhome as we were blocking them in, so I jumped in the seat, still dangerously half-asleep and drove off the ferry and straight into a high kerb, scraping the side of the van. This was getting beyond a joke but I was faced with the dilemma of getting past the M25 at night-time or having that hassle the next morning. I decided to press on until Oxford, where we parked up and slept for England. This has all made me realise that I am not going to drive my motorhome to anything more than one or two events next year. It is just not worth the hassle. By the time we get back to the Isle of Man tomorrow, we might as well have just stepped off a long-haul flight, as we'll be totally shattered.

Thursday, 5 July 2001

There was no point in doing any training, as it wouldn't have done me any good. I'd probably just about recovered by the weekend when we flew back to England for a public relations day with sponsors HM Plant, go-karting at the indoor centre at Silverstone. I'm no karter, and hadn't done it for three years, but try telling that to all the guests when I went and won the competition. I was riding pretty dirtily, cutting up the other drivers, so I thought it best to apologise during my acceptance speech, to ensure the PR stunt didn't backfire too much.

After a couple of nights in Burnley, combining Kathryn's 31st birthday and my brother Carl's 30th the previous night at a Greek restaurant in Colne, we flew down to Gatwick on Monday morning for the trip to America. Kathryn's dad, Martin, who lost her mum five years ago, was travelling with us along with one of his friends, Peter Ward, whose wife had also died with cancer just three months before. This pair had me in stitches for the whole of the trip. They are typical Northern blokes in their mid-fifties but have known each other for so long that they're like an old married couple – somebody compared them to Morecambe and Wise, which was pretty spot on.

'D'ya know, I've never known anyone eat as much as you,' Martin might say to Pete.

'Eee, you liar. How do you know? You're always asleep,' Pete would respond. And so it went on.

Kathryn was able to wangle Martin an upgrade for the Virgin

flight to San Francisco, and it was as though he'd never been on a plane before.

'Aye, I'll have a beer love,' he said, when the airhostess came round, then 'Aye, go on then, I'll have another if you're asking....' He's the only bloke I've known to have a beer with his cornflakes, as he did once when we were on holiday in Barbados, although he's not actually a big drinker – more of an early starter and early to bed man!

Other passengers had probably paid three or four thousand pounds for a bit of peace and quiet in first class, but that was all disrupted in the middle of one of the films when the airhostess came around one more time.

Martin had forgotten that he had headphones over his ears and bellowed at the top of his voice: 'No, I don't think I'll have Fosters this time. What else have you got, love?'

Kathryn and I were in tears in the seats in front.

'Dad, you're shouting a bit,' mouthed Kathryn to him.

'What? I can't hear you. What are you saying?' he shouted back.

I love Martin to bits but he's also a bit absent-minded and clumsy. There was a minor crisis when, after spending a couple of days in San Francisco, he left his passport in his hotel before travelling down to Monterey, where I'd headed straight from the flight.

The plan was to settle in and get relaxed, but a game of tennis with James on the Tuesday backfired when we both got fairly badly sunburned and, because we're not used to playing tennis on hard courts, our legs were aching from the jarring. So, two days before practice, we were both in the medical centre with sore legs like a pair of big girls. I'd also played in a pair of trainers that had shrunk when I washed them over in Misano. So, on top of everything else, I now had a bruised toe and dead toenail to contend with!

On another day we hired a four-wheeled bike, with four seats for everyone to pedal. We managed to fit five in – James, Dave Parkes, Colin and Stewart and myself – and had a great laugh mucking about along the coastal paths, where everyone else was either quietly walking or jogging. We tried to get up enough speed to lean it over round the corners but I had to get out and push to enable us to do a handbrake turn! That ride also proved a painful activity for the other four, because it was easy for your feet to slip from the pedals, and with everyone else still pedalling, the pedals whipped round to crack you on the shin. All in all, though, it was a relaxing few days, capped by a team visit to a brilliant Japanese restaurant that evening. I've never seen a chef crack eggs and then throw them into the air before cooking them under your nose.

Friday, 6 July 2001

I needed no reminding that this is quite a dangerous circuit. The last time I'd raced there was in 1998, when I was with Kawasaki as team-mate to Akira Yanagawa, who nearly died there after a bad collision with Doug Chandler. The crash dragged a lot of gravel across the track. I slid out on it but witnessed everything. The marshalls thought he had been killed and were shouting: 'He's dead! He's dead!'

It was a horrible experience, because other riders do not normally see the aftermath of a crash. I realised what a good job the marshalls do, because they must be severely traumatised by something like that. When I returned to the garage, Akira's wife, Emi, was asking me how he was. I knew that he'd suffered bad head injuries and, for all I knew, he was dead. But it turned out that a lot of the blood inside his helmet was the result of him biting through his tongue, as well as losing some teeth. He was still critical, however, and was airlifted to a San Francisco hospital, no one knowing whether he was dead or alive by the time the race was restarted.

Then, when we lined up on the start line for the next race, a massive screen was replaying footage of the crash, in full view of all the riders. It was the most distasteful thing I'd ever seen. I caught a glimpse of it from the corner of my eye, but had to look away immediately. That start was also marred by a big cart-wheeling crash, in which Aaron Slight was injured. By then everyone just wanted to pack up and go home. I know that I certainly didn't want to race – the only time I've had that feeling. Kathryn also found it all very traumatic and she felt creepy on arriving here to find that our hired motorhome was the same type that we'd shared with Akira that year – and was parked in the same place.

So, all of this was in the back of my mind before racing today, although I could counter it all with the fact that I have already been on the podium here, in 1996. However, I didn't have any reference points for when I came to the Corkscrew for the first time, as all the trees which used to surround the steeply sloping chicane had been removed. This is the only circuit in the world where they will not allow you to walk round in advance. They talk about America being free but that's rubbish. It's the most restrictive country I have ever been in. They are really strict on speeding – Troy Bayliss has been caught already – and you cannot smoke on the streets of California, which had our team in a panic. I was asked for ID in a bar, which is understandable. But Colin Wright is clearly not 21! The only reason they would give for stopping us walking the track was 'That's the rules. I don't make them, but that's the rules.'

I'd forgotten that it's quite a slow circuit, with mostly second gear corners. It is awesome, though, up and down all the way with so much character – as near to a roller-coaster ride as you can get on a bike. But right from the word 'go' we had a struggle with the gearing. I don't remember any problems from the last time we were here, but I know already that I'm going to have to compromise at a couple of corners. I got my first turn into the Corkscrew completely wrong and ran across the gravel. It was all feeling a bit weird.

I was fifth in the morning session, with a time of 1:27.008, compared to 1:26.583 from Ben Bostrom, who was already showing signs that he had the jump over everyone else through the Corkscrew. After trying different gearing in the afternoon, I was fifth again but still nine tenths of a second behind Bostrom, and while we were pretty happy with the set-up and the race tyres, the sessions were a bit 'bitty' and I didn't really get into a rhythm. Colin, therefore, took me to one side after the afternoon qualifying.

'Come on, let's try and get our acts together. Both you and Stewart are doing it again. We're getting into the routine of 'two laps, in, one click', 'two laps, in, one click', instead of leaving the bike alone and getting some laps under your belt,' he said.

It was another firm talking to, but not a bollocking. And we did need reminding, but this was the first time I'd seen him say anything to Stewart. The bikes had not been ready for the afternoon session and we were five minutes late out onto the track. It was mainly because I'd had a pair of forks that had gone faulty, as well as problems with the clutch. On top of that, James was also having problems, with the result that Stewart basically ran out of time and he couldn't delegate any of the tasks to other people. I'd not been bothered, because you could see that he was doing everything that was physically possible to make the start time, and five minutes does not really matter here nor there. But Colin thought it was serious enough to warrant raising his voice. I actually got dragged into it, which I thought was a bit unfair.

'You two, what was all that about at the start of the session?' Colin asked.

'Hang on a minute, I'm a rider. Can't you see I'm in my leathers? The bike's nothing to do with me,' I was thinking. And I could tell that Stewart was a bit taken aback and upset.

'I couldn't do any more than I did, and I did try to delegate some jobs,' said Stewart, standing up for himself.

I wasn't upset by what had been said, but I wasn't in a good mood when Motorex took about 10 of us out for an Italian meal that evening. I'd had a blinding headache all day and was just not in the mood for being polite. However, I don't like being an arse with Kathryn's dad around. I've spent loads of time with him, so hopefully he knows what I'm like by now, but I still felt obliged to make an effort.

Saturday, 7 July 2001

It was a similar story during today's qualifying, when I was there or thereabouts. But I've now sussed out that I don't really go for it on the first couple of days, as I'm more worried about race set-up. I don't even stick my neck out towards the end of the final qualifying, because I know that I'll always be faster in Superpole, and, if anything, I don't like being the last to go.

The only experiments we tried during the day were with a new front tyre that Dunlop had brought, which was slightly stronger and harder. I couldn't make my mind up about it, but finally agreed to use it for the races tomorrow. I didn't actually manage to improve on my time of yesterday afternoon and qualified in seventh, enjoying a relaxing wait before Superpole. There are no garages at Laguna, just a series of shady tented areas. The advantage, though, is that there are not as many journalists in your face while you're trying to prepare yourself.

James had qualified in tenth and set pole after his lap, half a second quicker than Yanagawa. I was pleased for him because he'd worked hard all weekend and had been on the pace. That had been the case a number of times during the year when he'd not been able to put in a good Superpole, resulting in the fact that he didn't get away with the leaders in the races. I realised that the other times had been pretty slow and I was quietly confident that I could knock a second off James' best time – and I managed 0.9! It helps to know that I've always saved the softest qualifier until Superpole and to know that at the start of that lap I'll have the best grip that I've had all weekend. That feeling allows you to turn the throttle so early.

The next few riders were all around 0.1 seconds up on me at the first split, but I'd ridden the next two sections perfectly, and they all slipped below me. The last man to go, Ben Bostrom, on his home track, was also up on the first split by the same amount. 'I've got pole here,' I thought, but then he went 0.3 seconds up at the next split. Although the gap dropped to 0.15 at the end of the lap, he beat me to pole position and I was left to start second on the grid. I knew, though, that I was going to be up there competing for the lead.

Until today we had eaten out every night and I didn't want to go through the rigmarole of waiting for service again tonight. I decided, instead, to get room service with Kathryn and fill our faces. But we'd forgotten what American portions are like, so when our five starters and my chicken dinner with side orders of broccoli and asparagus arrived, piled on a creaking trolley, we fell about laughing. The side order of broccoli alone would have filled me up!

Sunday, 7 July 2001

The warm-up session was a complete nightmare. The plan was for me to go for it for 20 minutes and do as many fast laps as possible. However, on my first lap, I nearly crashed six times and in places where I wasn't normally sliding. So I came straight back in.

'I think I'm leaking oil,' I told the team.

'Don't worry, I know what it is,' Stewart nodded, looking very serious before proceeding to let some air out of the back tyre.

'Dunlop wanted us to try something. We didn't tell you because we didn't want it to distract you from trying 100 per cent for the warm-up,' he said.

I was a bit annoyed that they hadn't bothered to tell me, but I think they know that I don't always give 100 per cent in the warm-up, and if I had known that I was still testing something, I probably wouldn't have gone for it. Dunlop had concerns that the soft race tyre was on the borderline of lasting the distance and wanted to try the same tyre, but with more pressure in it. When that extra pressure was released the feel returned to normal.

My start to the first race was the best of the year – I went off like a missile and it was weird to realise that there were no other wheels around, even entering the first corner. But I didn't enjoy the two laps in the lead, because I was constantly expecting someone to come past – although it didn't happen. I had expected to be up there, but not to be leading by so much and so early on in the race. My pitboard said +1 so I decided to just forget being tactical and put my head down. The lead increased to +1.3 at one point and, 15 laps into the race, I thought 'I'm going to win this. This is easy.'

Suddenly the gap was down to 0.8. Somebody had taken half a second out of my lead on one lap and I'd not made any mistakes. 'Aye aye, I've got company, here,' I thought. On the following lap, it had dropped further and my board said 'BOS'. The team tells me who is behind because different riders ride in different ways. For instance, Bostrom brakes late, whereas Corser doesn't. Corser will pounce if you make a mistake, but won't often out-brake you. Bostrom, on the other hand, will always have a good go up the inside. So, as soon as I knew it was Bostrom, I realised I had to brake later everywhere, with the result that my lap times fell because I was losing corner speed. That also allowed Corser to catch us up.

On the next lap at the Corkscrew I braked at the same point but must have been a bit harder, because the rear lifted ever so slightly, so I had to let the brake off for a split second. That meant I was entering the corner way too fast and ran wide. Sure enough, Bostrom came underneath me and pulled a lead straight away. After a couple of laps my lead on Corser started to increase and, when I knew I was pulling clear of him, I didn't feel threatened in second place.

I had to be happy with that result. Bostrom was on his home track and he gets a bit more out of his tyres than I do, as mine tend to shred a touch more. I think his riding style is somewhat ragged, but on the other hand, my tyres seem to wear more. It must be something to do with his suspension set-up.

The second race was a lesson in how not to start. I went into the first, second and third corners way too fast. Amazingly only Colin Edwards managed to come past when I went wide. It was bad enough that Bostrom had the chance to get away, but Edwards was the worst person to be behind because he knew that he wasn't as fast as we were and so would make it doubly difficult to get past. As a result I totally lost my rhythm and reverted to motocross riding, diving up the inside. It might have been exciting for me, but I wasn't giving my tyres a very easy ride. To make matters worse, Corser got involved and that meant Bostrom was pulling away all the time.

When I braked too late while diving underneath Edwards, pushing both of us wide, Corser nipped through and pulled a second on us. By the time I eventually passed Edwards, Corser was two seconds ahead. I perhaps closed in on him for a couple of laps before he started to pull away again to increase his lead to about three or four seconds. Then, without a threat from behind, and without any realistic chance of catching Corser in second, it was a pretty lonely race for me over the next 10 laps to take third place.

A lot has been said about the way that Corser is riding, with some people questioning his attitude and rumours that Aprilia will not be having him back next year, but it's very difficult to have an opinion on it. The bottom line is that he's easily beating his team-mate, Regis Laconi, every week and he's the only other guy out there on an Aprilia – and not a bad rider at that. Having said that, I sometimes feel that Corser is focused, but I also sometimes feel that he isn't. He's got plenty of money in the bank, so the edge might be going.

It was the first time I'd been on the podium for both races, outside England. And, all along, this is where I have wanted to be – up there with the leaders, but I couldn't quite work out whether or not the American supporters were impressed by my efforts. There was the usual hollering and whooping at the press conferences because Bostrom had won, but they also seemed to be cheering us just as much. People would come up to me and say things like 'Hey man, you were absolutely hanging out there' or 'Man, you're a demon!' I took them to be compliments – but at the same time wasn't 100 per cent sure what they were on about!

John Jones, the owner of our sponsors HM Plant, took 32

people out for a meal that night, including my brother, Carl and his girlfriend, Justine, and six other friends from Burnley. Carl, who works as a production manager for my dad's company, Moorplate, is the emotional one of the family. He is so keen for me to do well and I really appreciate the fact both he and my father are prepared to travel halfway around the world to watch me race. We are quite close, although not to the extent that we ring each other every day. It's like with my mates – we both know we're there when we're needed. Sadly Carl and Justine had to return home straight after the races because her stepfather had died of cancer.

Monday, 8 July 2001

A few of the group took the chance to do some sightseeing and shopping in San Francisco before the evening flight. I opted for a game of tennis with James – for one very good reason. The last time I was over here, the same chance to do some shopping with Kathryn in San Francisco came up - -but went horribly wrong. It scares me just thinking about it.

Kathryn had gone to the Diesel store across the road from the Ralph Lauren shop that I was in. When I'd finished there I went towards the exit to go and meet her. As I put my hand up to push open the swing doors, an old Red Indian woman, who looked like a witch, did the same thing at the other side of the glass. She opened the door for me to come through and stared at me in a confrontational way, but also as if she knew me. I didn't know what to do or say.

'It's you!' she said in an earnest and chilling voice before grabbing hold of my arm and pulling me closer to her face.

'You're the one!' she said again.

'Oh, oh! Weirdo! I don't want anything to do with her,' I

thought as I side-stepped her and ran into the Diesel store to find Kathryn.

' I've just had a right weird experience,' I said, my heart going ten to the dozen.

'What do you think of this, Neil? Blue or green?' replied Kathryn, typically concerned.

Then I spotted the old woman coming up the stairs, staring round for me.

'Bloody hell! That's her! She's followed me in here. Kathryn, you're going to have to do something – she's trying to get me,' I screeched before shooting off up the escalator.

The woman followed me onto every level of the store, always scanning round trying to see where I'd gone. By now I thought she was going to kill me. Whenever she spotted me she would stride purposefully towards me, but always at the same pace like in a cartoon. Kathryn was also following me, not knowing quite what to do and still finding it quite funny. After I'd reached the fourth floor there was no where else to go. Sure enough, the old woman was on the escalator. I was trapped and in a real panic, so I ran over to a big, beefy security guard.

'You're going to have to help me. There's an old woman trying to get me,' I spluttered.

'Hey, calm down man,' he said.

'You're going to have to get the police here,' I insisted.

'Show me this woman then,' said the security guard.

'There she is – over there,' I pointed.

The guard struggled to stop himself from laughing. I could see that he didn't consider the old woman to be as much of a threat as I now did. But, for all he knew, she could have had a gun and thought I'd murdered her son – or something like that. I couldn't believe that nobody else was taking this seriously. I wasn't going to get any help from the guard so I made for the stairs and ran down to the bottom floor, out onto the street and sprinted 200 yards up the road before hiding behind a lamppost, leaving Kathryn and the woman in the shop.

Within seconds she was back on the street, looking up and down for me.

'Oh no! I bet she's got unbelievable Red Indian powers,' I thought. 'She can probably smell me from here.'

Thankfully, she turned to walk the other way, but that didn't stop me from staying behind the lamp-post for another ten minutes, trying to attract Kathryn's attention. When she found me behind the post she suggested that we should go and get a juice at a bar around the block.

'You can forget that. We're getting the first taxi as far away from here as possible,' I said.

Brands Hatch – round 10

Friday, 26 July 2001

It's been the calm before the storm for the last few weeks. After Donington, I knew what was in store for me here, and up until last weekend, I'd tried to keep my diary pretty clear apart from a trip to Venice, to help Axo launch their new range of leathers. Tetsuya Harada, the Japanese 250cc rider was also there, along with Claudio Federici, a top Italian motocross rider, who was really friendly. It was a beautiful day and we had a chance to walk round the city, so it did not seem much like work.

Colin and Darrell had also been to Italy, to talk with Ducati about plans for next year. While everything they had to report was positive, there was still no confirmation that I'd be on a 2002 spec bike. Ducati also asked Darrell what they thought about me joining their full factory team.

GSE have the option on my contract for another year and Darrell knows that my only goal for next year is to win the world title. I still think that the best chance of that happening is by staying with GSE, on Dunlop tyres and with the latest engine.

So, in an ideal world, GSE will find the sponsorship and Ducati will provide those bikes for free. While this subject will keep cropping up in the media, I don't want to get bogged down with it until after the Assen round in September.

The public relations merry-go-round for this round started last weekend. First I was at Oulton Park for the British Superbike championship round, where I did a few pillion rides. Then, after a flying visit home, I was due in London on the Tuesday for a press conference at the London Eye, where I did a long interview for Grandstand. I have never known so many national newspapers turn up for one of these events. I've been to others when there have been just two journalists – and you know them both already. It was the first indication of just how hectic the next few days were to be.

Following a couple of nights at Darrell's home in Kent, I arrived at Brands yesterday to get settled in nice and early and help unload some of my stuff from the crates that had arrived back from America. There were also all the pre-race press events at the circuit itself.

One of the first riders I bumped into was John Reynolds. I have a lot of time and respect for John as a rider and a person. He's one of the nicest guys you'll meet – down to earth and totally modest – and someone who will ask genuine questions about you. And you'll never hear him bitching or singing his own praises. I got to know him more as a friend during an overnight ferry trip from Plymouth to Bilbao in 1994, when he was my team-mate for a one-off race on a 500cc for Padgett's. He's normally a pretty straight bloke but a few whiskies mellowed him and that's when I discovered there were two John Reynolds: the serious racer and the human being. You could also say there are two Neil Hodgsons, as I'm a much nicer guy at home than I am the circuit.

'Hi Neil. I'll try and do my best to keep out of your way on Sunday,' he said.

'That's okay then, if you're out the way that means I might be leading,' I laughed.

I know John, and just how modest he can be. I also know that he's a quick rider, who'll be wanting to win just as much as everyone else out there. But the fact that the other British riders were behind me was, in a nice way, adding to the pressure that was building. Even so, I couldn't really believe just how relaxed I've been feeling. Until today!

On the way from my motorhome to the garage this morning for the first session – a trip of just 400 yards – I must have been shouted at 30 times for autographs. However, I can't stop because, if I stopped for one, I would have to stop for everyone. Then, when you see a little kid, it's too difficult just to ride past on the scooter. So I try to get away with just signing one autograph, although it never works out that way and, before I've got through the 'Neil' of Neil Hodgson, I've got a queue building up and it's touch and go whether I'll make practice. It's not so bad when they have a pen and paper ready when I stop, but when they start scrambling around for any old thing to sign, it's very hard not to be ratty. So I was in a bit of a grumpy mood first thing. And this is just Friday – the day without the crowds.

I'm not recognised or stopped as much away from race meetings, although I am perhaps a little bit more conscious that my profile is bigger than it used to be a short while ago. For instance I might sign one or two autographs when I'm out and about on the Isle of Man, when last year there wouldn't have been anyone asking. However, if I was to walk through Heathrow Airport or Manchester city centre, I'd be really surprised if anyone was to stop me. After my brief flirtation with fame as a motorcycle racer I've already decided that I wouldn't like to be famous. I don't mind a bit of the trappings that go with it – more money and a bit of VIP treatment here and there. But then it gets out of control. So I'd hate to be a Madonna or a Robbie Williams and it's no wonder that they start going weird after a while. One group who will always recognise me, though, is the Halifax mob – they were sitting drinking opposite the garage from the very first thing this morning, of course – who cheered me up with their first chants of 'Hodddddg-son, Hodddddg-son!'

I struggled with grip this morning and was sideways in a couple of places in my second lap. You usually build up to going sideways, when you are pushing the bike so hard by mid-session that it starts to slide, but I realised that this was probably a track thing more than a bike thing. Having said that, we tried a total of four tyres in the first practice session, which is a lot for an hour. It was no surprise that three British championship guys, John Reynolds, Steve Hislop and Sean Emmett were the three fastest riders in that session.

It's not just the fact that they have raced here already this season, but that they were here only four weeks ago. I haven't been on my own bike for just over two weeks, so they were clearly going to be dialled into the track, shown by the fact that Sean Emmett was third. I finished fifth but was not surprised to be behind the likes of Hizzy. He's so full of confidence that I expect him to be on the pace all weekend. It's a weird feeling, wanting to beat a mate so badly. And the fact that he's on my old bike also means he would have one over me if he beats me.

Steve has had a lot of bad luck, in his personal and professional lives. He had an horrendous injury last year when he broke two bones in his neck in the corresponding race here last year. I'd unintentionally caused the crash, so I would have felt terrible if things had worked out even worse for him. At the time I remember thinking 'I'm going to have to live with this for the rest of my life if Steve's dead.'

We were all heading for the first corner when Chris Walker closed me in a touch and, not being able to see properly because someone was in front, I ran onto the steep kerb at Paddock. I momentarily lost control and so I had to stand the bike up, which always has a knock-on effect. Colin Edwards also picked his bike up and ran into Noriyuki Haga, before Steve was collected by them both.

He landed on his head and was instantly knocked unconscious before being flung through the gravel trap. Doctors missed the breaks on the X-rays, saying the shadows were down to a previous injury. It was not until Steve realised that he could no longer push with his left arm that a specialist discovered two vertebrae had crumbled away and the bones were rubbing on his nerve. By then he'd already attempted to compete in two British championship rounds and was told that, until he had an operation, a simple stumble might kill him.

He's fully recovered now and does seem to be more switched on this year than he has been recently. That's probably down to confidence, something he might not have always had a lot of. Now he's looking for a big pay day towards the end of his career and I hope he gets it, as long as it doesn't mean he has to beat me on Sunday.

The best thing about this morning's session, though, considering the fact that I'd been sliding around, was that most of the championship regulars, apart from Edwards in fourth, were the best part of a second slower than me.

I actually missed all the action between sessions, when Jamie Whitham and French rider Fabien Foret had a scrap in the pit-lane. It appears that they had got in each other's way and a few hand gestures turned into a bit of pushing and shoving before the helmets came off and a few blows were landed. I know how they must have been feeling because I'm notorious for being 'Mr Handbags At Dawn'. In 1998 I had a confrontation with Aaron Slight at Sugo in the final race of the year. After the race he had come alongside my bike and kicked me, claiming I was trying to help Fogarty win the championship. That wasn't the case; I'd just been sacked and I had my own point to prove, so it ended in a bit of pushing and shouting.

One year later, again in the final race of the year, at Donington, I was knocked off by Sean Emmett. I got up and walked over, expecting an apology. Instead, I received 'the finger'. So I ran over and hit him, which isn't the brightest thing to do when the other guy is wearing a helmet. Neither was it too bright to knock John Barton off in my first national race at the age of 17. He's about 6ft 6ins and, while I know now that he's really mild-mannered because he's my masseur on the Isle of Man, I thought he was going to kill me. These are not things I'm proud of, just heat of the moment things when you don't act as you know you should be doing.

We changed the suspension before the afternoon session because we hadn't altered the fork springs from Laguna and they were too soft for the uphill braking at Brands. It's as if you are braking into a brick wall, so the suspension bottoms out, and we were now down to two tyre choices. The English side of Dunlop have copied the Japanese tyre - a hard English compound but in the Japanese shape. I compared it against a genuine Japanese tyre and did my fastest race lap on the English one in the afternoon session. It's looking like it might be the race tyre, despite the fact that it hasn't been tried before. I also stuck in a qualifying tyre towards the end to finish the session fastest, which is where I wanted to be although the weather forecast is good for the whole weekend, therefore it's not likely that this session will have any bearing on the grid positions. All I need to do tomorrow is try and carry a bit more corner speed by decreasing the revs everywhere.

I was flat-out for a couple of hours after qualifying, with team debriefs and then an interview with Mary Anne Hobbs – remember her from Japan? She was back with a vengeance, and still wearing those same yellow leathers! But I was in such a good mood after the afternoon that I signed every autograph request on the way back to the paddock. Then I signed 100 prints as part of a deal that we'd struck up with an artist. I therefore, wasn't too chuffed when, thinking that I'd got all this out of the way, a few people actually turned up at the motorhome while we were watching the Big Brother finale, knocking on the door asking for signatures and telling me that 'I'd better do the double'.

I've had a word with SBK about this when I was in Venice for the Axo launch. Christina was telling me how much better the World Superbikes series was compared to the Grand Prix circuit, because the public have access to the riders.

What you don't realise is that you make it very difficult for the riders.'

'What do you mean?' she asked.

'When I come out of the back of my garage there are 20 people there who want my autograph. I don't have time to sign that many because all I've come out for is to change my helmet. So I end up being rude to people and that's not in my nature,' I added.

We do entertain and we do try and put on a decent show by doing things like the pit-lane walkabout, so at least when you are back in your own private space – the motorhome – it's not much to ask to be left alone for a few hours. Especially when we're watching the Big Brother finale!

This time last year at Brands coincided with the final night of last year's series, which we'd watched all the way through. Both of us loved Craig and thought he was really cool. So we were over the moon when he won. As he was leaving the Big Brother House, he was met by a girl suffering from Down's Syndrome and it was only then that we realised he had pledged his £70,00 prize money to her. Kathryn burst out crying and I was doing everything that men normally do to disguise the fact that they are nearly in tears – like coughing or pretending there was something in my eye.

This year we wanted Helen to win but, although she finished second, she was brilliant when she came out to face the fans – so natural. That really is proper television, I don't care what anyone else says. And, while I'm not superstitious, it has obviously clicked that the final of this year's show is on the Brands Hatch weekend again. There was also a firework display on the Saturday night last year so, if there's another one tomorrow night, I suppose that'll be a good sign.

Saturday, 27 July 2001

I was nervous today. It felt like a much bigger day than yesterday, probably because there were a lot more people here – around 30,000, and that figure obviously included the Halifax crew. Apparently they'd been sitting opposite the garage at 11 o'clock last night, when the team were pulling down the shutters, having returned from the pub still singing GSE to the tune of Let It Be. They'd warned Ashley that they would be there, ready and waiting, at 7 o'clock in the morning – which they were, just as they'd been in South Africa. What their insides and their livers, vocal chords and knees must be like after three days solid drinking, singing and dancing in this heat, I can't imagine.

But they worked wonders for both James and I. British crowds are a bit like sheep. Once they see someone leading, they

167

will follow, so when Halifax started singing, everyone else joined in and the crowd was really behind us all day. We'd also produced a lot of orange cushions for people in the crowd to sit on, trying to create a really colourful spectacle whenever we came out of the garage or down the start-finish straight. It worked to an extent today but should be better tomorrow.

It was clear, though, that England expected a result today. If I'd come tenth in qualifying in Germany, with Superpole to come, it would not have been a big deal. Here, today, I needed to give the fans something to shout about. The morning session did not go to plan, however. After a few laps we tried a new shock to see if I could hit the apex of the corners spot on but after six more laps I knew that it wasn't going to work, so we'd wasted around 25 minutes. The tyre choice was down to two: both were new English rubber. One had a slightly softer side wall, to increase the feel and grip on maximum lean. But we were also unsure whether to go with a 6inch or a 6.25inch rim. We still, therefore, had a lot to think about. Having done my runs on potential race tyres, I put on a qualifier but, lo and behold, Chili was following me down the pit-lane again, as he had done yesterday.

We both hesitated at the end and obviously couldn't see each other's expressions inside our helmets. But I knew that he was kind of asking 'Am I going to lead off or are you?' I always like a clear track ahead for my laps with qualifiers on, because that mimics Superpole conditions, so I cleared off. I can't see why other riders want to follow me round. Surely they should be trying to figure the track out for themselves and for their bikes? From that moment on I was completely unaware of whether he was there or not. I didn't manage to better my time so tried a harder qualifier and, with six seconds of the session remaining, set the second fastest time, a tenth of a second behind Colin Edwards.

The break between sessions was frantic again, but I'd learned the lesson from Donington; I made a beeline for my motorhome where Kathryn had made some pasta, which was not quite cooked, with some plain tomato sauce that was cold because the microwave wasn't working. It was not exactly a feast fit for a king but at least I had something inside me! After an SBK signing session and pit-lane walkabout, followed by the first of two massages for the day, I scrounged 40 minutes in the motorhome to myself before I was back in my leathers.

We made a few changes for the afternoon, increasing the offset from 28 to 29, because the bike still wasn't turning properly into corners. It was also still diving quickly on the front fork, so we made the forkspring heavier once more and added some more oil. Colin also wanted me to start the session on the second bike, to put some more mileage on it and also to save my race bike until tomorrow. However, it had new forks in and didn't feel right at all.

'I can't tell the difference with anything. There's something wrong,' I told them.

Instead, I went back out on the number one bike, which had all the same changes. After another five laps I realised that I didn't like the changes, but I knew that to change everything round again would waste another 20 minutes or so. I was also aware, though, that I'd been wasting my time just carrying on and riding round.

'Look guys, I know I need to be testing tyres, but we're going to have to change it all back, because it's shit,' I said. It was a big decision, but it was my decision because to ride round doing 1:28 second laps wasn't going to do my confidence any good, and I'm paranoid about the tyre choice because of what happened in Italy and Germany.

'Has anyone else done race distance on any tyres yet?' I asked Higgy.

'No, you've done the most with 16 laps,' he replied.

'Great! So am I the one doing all the donkey work for everyone else,' I thought. It's annoying but there's no way you can have any secrecy because it would be so easy for the tyre boys to let stuff slip over a beer back at the hotel.

When we changed everything back, the bike felt great, but I was still struggling a bit through the final split and was a tenth down on Edwards through it. At first I thought it might have been that my bike was less powerful, then I figured it out for myself that I wasn't carrying enough corner speed through Clearways. So towards the end of the session, with a race tyre on that had done 15 laps, I tried letting the brake off earlier and was able to get on the throttle more smoothly, stopping the fishtailing of the back wheel. I finished that session third behind Edwards and Ruben Xaus.

Right now, because Superpole doesn't mean a lot, it's looking like the men to beat tomorrow are going to be Edwards, Hislop and possibly Corser. I can't see Bostrom doing anything unless he pulls his finger out, because his race times have been poor – probably a second too slow, but you never know. Hopefully Steve won't have the burning desire because he won't want to risk his lead in the British championship, though if he really wants to win tomorrow, he'll be very hard to beat. You are never too sure with Edwards. He has been qualifying well, but not really threatening in the races.

Troy Bayliss was out three riders before me for Superpole. As he came round Clearways it was obvious there was smoke coming from the bike and that he was leaking oil. He should have been black-flagged because you are then heading for some very fast third-gear corners. This track is too dangerous in my opinion but the most dangerous spots are the places where you should not come off. For instance you are probably doing

140mph in the dip before Dingle Dell, where you've only got 1.5metres run-off. That's fine normally, but if suddenly spill all your oil when you are leaning over then you are going down – and where is there to go? It's always through freak accidents that people get killed, so while I don't know who was to blame, I was annoyed that Troy was allowed to carry on and couldn't watch it.

'If he crashes there, he's dead or seriously hurt,' I thought. 'Black-flag him for God's sake.'

The worst thing that might have happened to him if he'd been stopped would have been to start one row back on the third row. As it is, he will be on the fourth row, because his bike was so slow. Riders do rely on other people to make these decisions. We have got tunnel vision and are not going to pull in on the suspicion that the bike's leaking oil, especially if you're leading the world championship. It was obvious Troy was going to carry on regardless without those flags. There didn't appear to be any oil on the track, though, so that was not a worry.

Hislop was on before me, so I wasn't aware what time he'd done and what I had to beat. But I didn't get the first two corners right and lost all momentum in the middle of the straight when the bike hit a false neutral. I thought I'd blown it, so I tried to get my head down and ride as hard as I possibly could. I went through Dingle Dell as fast as I had done all weekend and got the last corner perfectly. Even so, when I saw my time, I was sure that it would be around a fifth of a second too slow. The crowd was cheering, though, so I pulled a few wheelies and returned to the pit-lane to find out I was first, with only Edwards to go. And he has not really been pulling it off during Superpole.

When he crossed the line the crowd started to cheer and everyone looked straight at me, so I knew I was on pole, but I can't help but think though, that they're not cheering for me –

it's as though they're still cheering for Carl Fogarty. For so long I have been in his shadow, and rightly so. When I've won four world titles, then don't talk to me about Carl Fogarty. As his team-mate, I've always been aware of this adulation for him. Now that it's for me, it's really weird. I almost have to look over my shoulder to check that he's not behind me and that they really are cheering for me. It is very hard to take in.

It hit me again after the press conferences. Dread, who make the team clothing and merchandise, had arranged for me to do a signing of t-shirts and hats at their tent. The queue was absolutely massive and I couldn't get my head round the fact that families had bought four lots of Hodgson t-shirts and hats. Then I experienced the coolest thing I have ever seen in racing.

Seven guys were wearing orange wigs, silly glasses and orange boiler suits, each showing a big black letter – H through to N – in the style of lettering that I have on my leathers. So when they stand in line it spells HODGSON. But here's the best bit. There was another bloke, not in a boiler suit, but still wearing an orange wig. He walked round to the first bloke, who was wearing H, and knelt down. He was the 'kneel' in Neil Hodgson. Kathryn thought he must have tagged along at the last minute so they came up with that as an afterthought. The time and effort they must have put into it was incredible and I demanded that they allowed me to have my picture taken with them. It's that Fogarty thing again, but it felt brilliant. I was so genuinely, mind-blowingly proud. Gaining pole position meant nothing compared to seeing that.

For every genuine fan, though, you also get the idiots and later on Kathryn was stopped by a few drunkards. The first wasn't too bad.

'Are you Neil Hodgsshon's girlfren. He'll win one tomorrow,' he said.

'Well let's hope he wins them both,' she said.

Then his mate chimed in. 'He won't. He won't you know,' he persisted. 'Boshtrom'll win both. I know.'

'Are you a fortune teller then?' asked Kathryn. But that one didn't have a chance to reply before the third got in on the act.

'No, Boshtrom won't win. Edwardsh'll win both.' And so on and so on…!

She left them to it, and went for a run around the track, not knowing that the marshalls were radioing to each other that there was a streaker running round. When they all kept shouting to her 'I see you've got your clothes back on', she didn't have a clue what they were on about until one of them let her in on the secret. And she swears she was only running naked through the wooded sections!

Meanwhile, I'd come face to face with a real fortune-teller. And after my experience in California, I was a bit worried. She had long, untidy hair and a long dress and said:

'Good luck for tomorrow, but you won't need it.'

'I always need a bit of luck,' I smiled back.

'Not this time. It's in the cards!'

Thanks! I'll hold you to that,' I laughed nervously, shaking her hand. Then, finally, I was able to get back to the relative peace and quiet of the motorhome.

Everyone prepares on the night before a race in his own way. There is no script that has to be followed. I know that at this moment in time I am physically and mentally exhausted. Yet Jamie Whitham is on stage playing for his band, The Po Boys, out in one of the fields. How he manages to do that on the night before a race I will never know. I've seen him play a number of times and know that he puts a lot of physical effort into it and sweats like a pig. I suppose he only has one race tomorrow, which does make a difference, and if that's what makes him relax, then good luck to him. But I couldn't think of anything worse.

It's typical of James, though, as he doesn't do things by halves. He is the salt of the earth, like no other rider and perhaps the funniest person I know – a lot of it taking the mickey out of himself. In fact, I'd go so far as to say that I sometimes don't like being in his company because he is so witty that it makes me realise just how boring I actually am. I might be just about to tell a story, when he'll chirp up with one of his own. So I stop myself in my tracks, deciding not to compete with him. It's just impossible to tell a joke in his company because he'll have already had everyone in stitches talking about something trivial like eating a custard pie.

He has a zest for life that everyone could learn from. I didn't know him too well before he suffered from cancer but I think he was just the same before that. His wife Andrea is no different – a naturally funny person and the perfect complement for their double act. We haven't seen them this weekend, but that's not unusual. We might not see either of them for a couple of meetings and then they'll come round to the motorhome on consecutive nights – and we love it when they do. He actually helps me relax before a race, because he takes my mind off racing. Jamie can be talking about something as mundane as mountain biking in the pouring rain – but something weird will always have happened to him. If I go mountain biking, it's okay. But Jamie will get lost and spend six nights in an old haunted cottage and manage to escape by making a tyre out of some bramble! He'd make a brilliant after-dinner speaker.

Sunday 28 July

My early night did not do me much good as I woke up at 5am, with demons rampant inside my head. I couldn't stop going through different race scenarios – mainly what might go wrong. I wasn't trying to psyche myself up, quite the opposite. I wanted to get back to sleep but I just couldn't. I now know that I have never been nervous before, until this morning. This was proper nervousness.

Last year at Brands was a big weekend for me. But the crowd would not have been devastated if I hadn't won. Back then, I'd placed a lot of pressure on myself, but this time around it was a different kind. Not only is there the personal pressure again, this time there is also that of an expectant crowd. I could not even eat my breakfast. I struggled to eat a tiny bit of muesli, but knew that I'd not had enough. I asked Kathryn to make me some toast and jam but I couldn't even eat that. I suppose this must be what it's like to be anorexic – I simply could not face eating food.

Arriving at the garage didn't help. The plan to turn the crowd into an orange mass by providing them with orange cushions had worked. The grandstand looked like they were supporting the Dutch national side – it was just a sea of orange and it was obvious from a very early stage that there was going to be a massive crowd. The flags were out in force and one opposite our garage – The Orange versus the Lemons - - was about the best.

The first cheer went up when I arrived in the garage and from then on they pretty well cheered my every move, the chorus being led by the Halifax mob, of course. But the warm-up session did not go to plan. We tried taking 3mms off the ride height because the back end was 'chattering' slightly in some of the faster corners. It didn't work, so I had to come back in. The bike was better when it was changed back to the original setting.

Then it was just a waiting game. The butterflies had more room to flap around in my stomach, because I still had only been able to nibble at my food, but the time just flew by until the first race. Before I knew it, I was lining up at the front of the grid, right next to the crowd at the other side of the fence. Foggy came and crouched down at the side of my bike, which I appreciated because he was there to work with the Ducati factory team really. Although it meant that there were even more cheers, it did serve to take my mind of the race for a second. I think that having been in that situation before, he realised exactly what I was going through and perhaps it's what he would have wanted in a similar situation. It must have looked like he was giving me last minute advice. He was actually telling me what he'd had for dinner the previous night and where he was going on holiday.

'God knows how you put up with this for years,' I said. Carl laughed knowingly. And then it was down to me.

My start was good but, right from the first corner, I thought I was leaking oil. Every time I touched the throttle on maximum lean the bike was sliding. It was horrible to ride.

'That's it, my race is over and I've not even completed a lap,' I thought.

Soon, though, the English Japanese-style tyre with the softer side wall started to find more grip, although not much. I really struggled to get past Edwards and then, when I did, I also struggled to increase my advantage and he got me back. Bostrom had little problem pulling past us and, when the race was stopped after a horrendous-looking crash involving James Haydon and Robert Ulm, with their bikes catching fire but both riders walking away, he had a 1.6second advantage.

The race was restarted, with grid positions decided by standings in the first section of the race – so I was now third on the new grid. We'd decided to copy the tyre that Bostrom had used - the Japanese one. That's not always also the wisest thing to do, but we had little choice. The problem was that we didn't know whether it was just a faulty tyre, or the wrong tyre. Straight away, though, I knew that we'd made the right choice.

My lap times were up by half a second and this time I managed to keep up with Bostrom. Even when I was leading my board was showing -1.6, so I knew that he was right behind me and I had too much work to do to overturn that deficit and win the race on aggregate.

Fred Clarke, who does the public address, got carried away and initially gave the impression that I'd actually won overall, but I wasn't getting carried away. I knew that I was second, so there was no reason to be pulling wheelies or any other extravagant celebration. I wasn't totally fed up and I don't want to sound like a spoilt brat, but this was built up to be my weekend, and second place was not what I had in mind. I had probably keyed in a victory, as I had at Donington and probably will do for Lausitzring and Misano next year. If I'd used the right tyre from the start, though, I think I would have been leading when the race was stopped and then who knows what might have happened in the 15-lap dash.

It was incredible how Bostrom had upped his game on race day but it looks as though he's got a great relationship with his chief engineer, a bit like I have with Stewart. Sometimes he looks nowhere in practice, but he's probably using the time to test rear tyres for the race. Not only is he riding well and really smooth, he's not making any mistakes. The bike fishtails on him but it's all totally under control and he doesn't miss apexes. I thought I was faster than he was through a couple of corners, though. He was quicker than I was through the left-hander after Dingle Dell, as well as out of Druids. There, I was opening up the throttle with my back end sliding and feeling a bit lazy. His bike doesn't slide, so he's able to drive away and pull a slight gap on every straight.

That's not all he's pulled recently. His new tall model-looking American girlfriend, Cat, goes everywhere with him, and they usually look pretty much at each other most of the time. I didn't see this, but they were actually snogging on the line before the start of the second race. In fact I don't know of any other couple who kiss so much in public. It's not for me and Kathryn, but I suppose it's whatever works for them and, anyway, it's what happens behind closed doors that counts. We are probably really lovey-dovey in private but, when I'm racing, I don't ever think 'Oh, doesn't Kathryn look beautiful today!' I have no room for any other emotion. Having said all that, I really like Ben. He's very modest, especially for an American and a good-looking guy – who might be expected to be more full of himself.

I'd only managed to eat a bit of pasta and have a massage during the break and was still as nervous as hell, so it was up to Chili to lighten the mood before the start of the second race for me. It's not like Chili to miss a chance to play up to the crowd so, minutes before the warm-up lap, he strode up to my bike, whipped off my cap and replaced it with his own. It perhaps wasn't what my sponsors wanted at the highest-profile race of the year, but it made me laugh.

I got away well and, with Bostrom in the back of my mind, just tried to nail it in case he'd had a bad start and was stuck in the pack. Things like tyre conservation went out of my mind. The team had changed the front forks to make it rebound quicker and this was an improvement – but not enough. I was surprised, though, when someone stuck in a 1:26 second lap to eat into my lead, as I'd just stuck in a 1:27.1 – one of my best of the weekend on race rubber. And I knew that it had to be Bostrom. When he overtook I didn't try to attack back straight away. Instead I decided to have a good look at him because he'd had the chance to study me for a while. In any case, I was riding on the limit. But with six laps to go drops of water started to appear on the screen. There had also been a few spots in the first race but I didn't think anything of it and actually forgot to mention it to the team as it could be down to nothing more than a bit of brake fluid. Then a lot more water appeared on the screen and I thought 'Oh no! It's raining. They're going to stop the race. I'm not going to get a chance to attack him.' By now the water was streaming down my visor and I glanced at the temperature, which was 117 degrees, and realised that the head gasket had blown and the bike was leaking water. I knew exactly what had happened because we had the same problem last year, when I was beaten by John Reynolds at Snetterton. I also knew that my race was over, although I expected the bike to continue without its normal punch, so I pushed as hard as I could and started to make mistakes.

I was devastated when I was riding round on the last lap. The support was absolutely fantastic and everyone seemed ecstatic. But I felt that I'd let them down. All weekend everyone had been telling me 'You're going to do the double, you're going to do the double'. Two second placings wasn't what they had in mind, but I didn't want to spoil the mood by going into a sulk.

Months and months ago, when I was killing time with Kathryn at Manchester Airport, I walked past The Sock Shop and spotted some Union Jack boxer shorts and socks. Immediately I thought 'That's me sorted for Brands Hatch'. The plan was, of course, to throw my leathers into the crowd and reveal the shorts after I'd won. But it didn't seem to matter to the fans. I'd already decided on Friday that I was going to throw them to the Halifax mob. There's probably a million people more deserving than they are, but they are just so unbelievably mental that I wanted to show my appreciation. When I hurled them over, two of the mob got into a fight over them and one ended up with just a knee slider. So, when I bumped into them later in the paddock – almost literally in their case – I promised that guy I would give him another set when they turned up at Imola. And I'm a man of my word.

After standing on the rostrum in my boxers – with my cycling shorts on underneath of course – it was straight into the sweaty minibus for the short trip to the SBK tent for the press conference. If the temperature wasn't high enough already it was raised a few more degrees when Bostrom's girlfriend hopped in and got straight back into some more snogging. But the drive did give me the chance to tell him just how well I thought he was riding. That's five wins on the trot for him and nobody has done that since Foggy in 1993, so you have to take your hat off to him.

By the time all the public relations stuff was out of the way I was absolutely exhausted and felt sick and almost ready to faint. After a shower I felt a lot better and went back to our hospitality to be polite and to try and spend a bit of time with the team. It was hard work, though, because I was exhausted and I had nothing to celebrate. While I had just a couple of shandies, my mum was in bed before 10 o'clock – because she didn't want to show me up. She wasn't paralytic or falling about, I just knew what was coming. Whenever anyone asks a question about me she'll start on 'Oh, he was a sickly child' or 'I always knew he had enough talent to be a top sportsman.' But she's a proud mum and that's what proud mums do. Trouble was I just didn't feel all that proud of what I'd done today.

Oscherleben – round 11

Thursday, 30 August 2001

Kathryn has been hard at work on the wedding arrangements during the break since Brands Hatch. She found a lady in Colne, a town near Burnley, who makes personalised invitations and Kathryn designed ours so that when the envelope is opened rose petals fall out. On the back was an inscription 'Exclusively designed by Art Inc'. The replies had started to trickle back to us when, one morning, in amongst the post was the tattiest envelope that I'd ever seen, with bits of grass, leaves and soil sellotaped to it. On the back it read 'Exclusively designed by Whit Inc'. I nearly fell about laughing but didn't open it because Kathryn was away on a flight to Barbados. When she did open it, there was more muck stuffed inside, and on the section asking for any special dietary requirements, James had written 'Pie and chips'. It was typical Whitham.

It was nice to return to this kind of normality after the whirlwind weekend that was Brands Hatch. From there, after spending the Sunday night in the motorhome, we drove to the GSE yard to leave the motorhome and then on to Darrell's home near Ashford before catching a flight to Nice at teatime. Aaron Slight was on the same flight, returning to his home in Monaco from Brands. I hadn't seen him for a while, so it was nice to catch up. I was left with the feeling, though, that he was frustrated by the fact that he'd had to retire through a lack of opportunities rather than having made the decision himself. He had suffered a brain haemorrhage at the end of 1999 and, although he'd recovered from that operation, the offers to ride were no longer out there. He may well get back into racing and I think he would still be competitive. I don't know whether he would win races but he could probably finish in the top five.

Our week in the South of France at Darrell's villa was probably the best holiday I've ever had. It normally takes me a full week to wind down and relax. Here, I switched off straight away. I needed the break so badly, as my batteries were at rock bottom after Brands. The weather was fantastic and it was lovely just to chill out with Darrell and his family, wife Michelle and kids Josh and Nadine, around the pool. You might expect that having two young children around would not be the most relaxing experience. But they were as good as gold and we did not know they were there most of the time. And then, when I was feeling more playful, they were there to muck around in the pool with. We also had time to chew the fat and put the world to rights over a few drinks. Darrell's whole life revolves around racing and, while I am passionate about it, I usually try to get away from the subject when I'm on holiday with Kathryn. But, for a change, it was great to talk to someone who knew what he was talking about. We slagged loads of people off – and complimented a lot as well – in a nice, merrily drunk way.

We also went over to visit Troy Bayliss, at his £2million rented apartment in Monaco. Soon after I first met Troy, at the second race of 1999 at Thruxton, Troy and his wife Kim got completely 'wrecked' and decided to stay at the track after the races, while I wanted to drive back to Burnley after a bad weekend. However, Kim kept hugging me and slurring:

'Don't go! We really want you to shtay. Look, I've made you something to eat.'

'No, really Kim, I have to be getting off,' I insisted.

'You're going nowhere. Come here and shee what I've made.'

So I went into their motorhome to see a frying pan filled with the most disgusting-looking lasagne you could imagine. The decision was made – I was definitely going home. Ever since then I've ribbed Kim about her cooking, promising that I would never eat anything that she had made. I was a bit apprehensive, therefore, when Kim revealed she'd cooked a Thai meal for us. It was, of course, absolutely fantastic – better than anything I've ever had in a Thai restaurant. To cap it all, Monaco was staging the World Fireworks championships so we were looking out from the balcony over a magnificent display.

We were also all drunk as skunks, having had the best part of a bottle of gin, but Troy doesn't like to talk about racing as much as Darrell and I. We're obviously not going to talk tactics together, because he's a rival. At one point, when it looked as though the conversation was heading down the road of the current championship, he said to Darrell: 'Enough of that now.' It's not that he won't talk about bikes, it was because he was leading the championship and he didn't want reminding of the pressure, and I can totally understand that.

It was good to spend time with Troy – and his family. I absolutely love his three-year-old daughter Abbey. Normally, if we are in a room with kids, they'll rush up to Kathryn and hold her hand. But Abby adores me and will always hold my hand before Kathryn's. She's so sweet and Mitchell, his son, is just a miniature Troy who looks like and does everything like his dad.

The late nights soon caught up with me, especially when I went on a bike ride with Troy. He is really fit and into his road cycling in a big way. I class myself as really fit, but someone who only does a moderate amount of cycling. Troy sold it to me as 'a big ride – but nothing stupid', we were going to a gorge with rapids that was four hours away. The plan was for the girls to drive to meet us there with a picnic. We set off at 8am to try and miss the real heat and maintained a steady pace for the first hour and a half, before I got a stitch.

'That's unusual,' I thought. 'I can't remember the last time I had a stitch. It'll go away in a minute.'

But it got progressively worse and Troy started to pull away a bit (not for the first time this year!) It wasn't that he was going any faster, just that I must have slowed. I tried to push harder but seemed to be using only half of my lung capacity and my breathing was becoming pretty heavy. I knew I would have to tell him to stop, but left it to the last possible minute out of macho pride.

But soon enough was enough. 'Troy we're going to have to stop. I've got a weird stitch. It really hurts when I breathe in,' I gasped.

'That's okay mate. No worries,' he said. 'We'll see how you feel after ten minutes.'

The stitch didn't go away but we agreed to take it at a steady pace for another hour and a half before we stopped for a drink and a croissant.

'It's only another hour from here – up a bit of a climb,' Troy assured me. Little did I know that the last time he'd tried to do the ride he had to stop halfway and get a lift to the gorge. It was actually two hours away, uphill all the way and a climb of another 1,000 metres. I'd run out of water and was totally dehydrated. This was supposed to be fun! It took the girls two hours to drive there and even Troy had felt it.

'That was a good ride,' he said, which for him translates as 'I'm knackered '.

The stitch had stayed with me all this time and was still there the next morning. By now I was so paranoid that I was telling Kathryn that I had cancer. When it eventually went my theory changed to blaming a fishbone. We'd had fish the previous night and I had swallowed a few bones. Maybe one had stuck somewhere and pricked a muscle into spasm.

'Just keep an eye on him Troy. We've had this fishbone nonsense before but I'm a bit worried about his fitness,' laughed Darrell before our next bike excursion.

It must have been in the back of my mind as well, because I threw myself into training when I returned to the Isle of Man. I also had a fair few public relations commitments, including a photoshoot of me jumping my 996 race replica on the roads around the Isle of Man, an interview for the Superbike magazine, a dealer weekend in Bridgewater, another in Grimsby and a charity ball in Newcastle for HM Plant. So all in all I was fairly busy before travelling to Germany.

The drive was straightforward – until we reached Oschersleben, a small town between Hannover and Magdeburg just over the border of what used to be East Germany. It only took us eight hours to reach here but then we spent the best part of another hour trying to find the bloody track. We either followed signs to the wrong part of the track or followed the right signs for the paddock, right up until the final turn where the key sign was missing. Then we drove two miles out of Oschersleben and had to phone the team for directions before doing a U-turn, which is never easy on winding country roads in this massive motorhome.

Having arrived, feeling frustrated and a bit stupid, it was good to see the team again. It didn't take long for the crack to start with James. Normally he is far better prepared than I am, but here he was faffing about trying to find his helmet and gloves.

'Ah, see! A couple of good results at Brands and it's gone to his head,' I laughed.

And it wasn't the only thing to have gone to his head. James had arrived here with blond streaks in his hair, which I didn't think looked too bad. Colin didn't agree, as he seems to have a thing about streaks. He was mucking around with James, saying he was going to shave it off, although I think there was a serious point to it. Colin actually shaved a line at the back with beard trimmers, which looked even worse, so James told him to shave it all off. That left little spots of blond dye here and there – a kind of leopardskin effect.

The funny thing was, though, that Colin had approached a decent 250cc rider called Scott Smart – who had a deliberate leopardskin hairstyle – at the end of the 1996 season, asking him to attend a meeting with Kawasaki with a view to taking the factory superbike ride for the following year. When Scott agreed, Colin said:

'You'll be doing something about your hair, though, first. Won't you?'

'No, I'm leaving it as it is,' Scott replied.

'That's fine. Just don't bother turning up to that meeting,' Colin told him.

So that was a good young rider's chance to break into superbikes blown out of the window. If he's sitting at home watching pictures of the World Superbikes, Scott will be thinking 'I didn't miss out on that ride because of my hair at all. James Toseland is riding for Colin Wright and he's allowed a leopardskin look. They must not have fancied me for some other reason.' I'm not sure how I would have reacted if it had been me, and not James. At the end of the day, though, Colin runs the team and treats the riders as he sees fit – and you can either like it or lump it. That might sound a bit harsh but Colin is fantastic with James and I. He's a great motivator and certainly gets the best out of me.

To date, I have really loved working with this team. As far as I know, though, the situation regarding next year has not changed since Brands Hatch. However, Roger also had a meeting there with Neil Tuxworth, the Castrol Honda team manager. They are obviously interested, although it seems as though there's a bit of a political battle between their European arm and the Japanese end as to whether to go for me or to retain Tady Okada. Roger might have talked figures with them, but he didn't mention that to me. I'm disappointed that there has been no progress with Ducati, but not surprised. The whole of Italy seems to close down during August, so there has been no one around to provide the answers that we need.

From what I can gather, sponsors are no longer the main issue for GSE. I think half the budget is in place for next year. At this time last year there was nothing in place. They are now just looking for someone to provide the £1 million or whatever it needs to take over the whole image of the team as title sponsor. The key thing is now the level of support that Ducati are going to provide and I think there's a meeting planned for later this weekend. But I'm not going to be worrying about that. Racing starts tomorrow morning and my main priority is to get round the track as fast as I can and win two races on Sunday. If that happens people will be knocking on my door, so I won't have to worry about next year. I'd only be worrying if I was desperate to get a foot in the door somewhere, in which case I'd be on the phone to Roger every day.

Friday, 31 August 2001

I was bound to be at a disadvantage here, having never raced at the circuit before whereas all the other riders had been here last year for the first time. It means I'm playing catch-up from the start of the weekend. But, all things considered, today was pretty good. I might have been a bit fed up after the second session, when I didn't go as quickly as expected on a qualifier, but I was only a second off the pace throughout the day and that was as good as could have been expected. I'm realistic enough to know that I'm not going to be up there right from the off.

The morning session was frustrating in that we didn't even get any proper wet practice, as the track was always drying and some corners were properly dried by the time we went out. I started out on a new wet tyre but had a few strange slides straight away.

'Can we not just put a normal wet in?' I asked when I came into the garage. 'I've not been on my bike for a month and I want to remember what it feels like.'

The normal wet tyre felt better but I decided that, instead of wasting laps, I'd get one step ahead of the others by going straight for intermediates as the track was drying so quickly. That was a mistake. I should have put slicks in straight away. So, after two laps on intermediates, I was back in the box asking for slicks. However our slicks had only been on the warmers for five minutes because Colin had expected the whole session to be wet.

The guy who looks after tyres is Ashley Parkes, who joined the team this year, which couldn't have been easy for him because it's a pretty close-knit outfit. He's a long-standing friend of Colin's and, although he has a bit of a 'gofer's' job, he's been given more responsibility with tyres and spares because he's so reliable. Although he's pretty quiet, Ashley thinks a lot about what he does say. If I've done well in a race, he'll wait until all the chaos has died down and catch me in a quiet moment in the corner of the garage, look me right in the eyes, and say: 'Really well done there mate.' And you know that he really means it.

Colin told me to go back out on the intermediates until the slicks had reached their proper temperature. It did feel much better for the ten minutes that I managed on slicks and I finished the session third, 0.8 of a second behind Troy Bayliss and just slower than Colin Edwards with a time of 1:34.445. I was buzzing. On first impressions, the final quarter of the track seemed really nice and flowing, but the first part was very tight and rubbish, just two horseshoe corners followed by a sequence of fast lefts on a bumpy surface. When you come to a new circuit you are always excited in the hope that the surface will be smooth, and I think that they should always give the track time to settle before racing on it – especially with cars. My theory is that if cars are braking heavily on a new surface, especially on a hot day, they can disrupt the tarmac and cause it to ripple. It's probably a load of nonsense but it seems logical!

We had not managed to gain any meaningful data in the morning session so there was nothing much to change for the afternoon. Our set-up, not having been here before, was based on the walk round the track that we'd had last night. We felt that because the layout was similar to Lausitzring, we would use that set-up as a base. It turned out that the offset and gearing were not quite right, but I didn't want to spend the whole of the afternoon session in the pits making small changes, as I needed to learn the track first and foremost. In some corners, though, I was right on the bottom of the stroke or on the oil and I couldn't carry on riding like that without the risk of crashing. So Stewart took a bit of oil out on a couple of occasions because, on a track with long horseshoe corners, you want to have the front ride as low as you can in a neutral position. I'd also heard a bit of a rattling and looked down to see if anything was hanging off. Back in the garage I realised that the chain was slack. That's not something I'd get upset about unless it happened three or four times, but I think that Pete got a gentle reminder from Colin not to let it happen again.

One of the challenges today for me was to try and work out the correct gearing. To do that you just have to go as fast as you can without scaring yourself. You also have to watch what the other riders are doing and, if you realise that you are carrying a lot of revs at one particular corner, look to see if the others are running a gear higher. If that doesn't work for you, then you have to look at changing the gearing. I managed to follow Corser for half a lap, knowing he was on the pace, which proved useful. And Roger Burnett was out on the track at different points, also gauging what the others were up to. I ended the session in 13th but was never in a sweat over whether I would finish in the top 16.

My fastest lap was actually the third on the qualifier, which is bizarre. I think people were beginning to wonder whether I was testing race distance on that tyre! The tyre had actually deteriorated as normal but I was so angry that I'd cocked up the first two attempts on it. However, at a new circuit, you will make mistakes. You are not going to be inch perfect on your first lap and, at the moment, I'm metre perfect. Compare that to somewhere like Donington or Brands, where I'm millimetre perfect and know that if someone put a coin down on my line, I would run over it on every lap.

It's a similar thing with braking points. At some tracks I will use a marker to determine when I hit the brakes. But, more often than not, it's an instinctive thing. I'm not being big-headed when I say that the ability to hit that spot every time, when you are travelling at 160mph, is one of the things that makes me a good bike racer. I don't necessarily need to have a 100m board at the side of the track to tell me when I should be braking. At a new track, though, I would use more markers than normally. I might start off at the 200m board and think 'That's way too early'. Then I'd try 150m between the two boards and think 'Now we're getting there'. After trimming it down and becoming used to the look of the corner I can forget about the board altogether and rely on my instincts.

The riders had arranged a meeting with Peter Ingley, our representative, in the evening. Out of the top 15 superbike riders only around 10 turned up, which was a bit annoying, with Ben Bostrom the most noticeable absentee. Peter explained that he had not been able to find a sponsor to fund his expenses and wage. I don't expect anybody to work for nothing and the others agreed that the top 15 riders would pay an amount, the next 15 a smaller amount, and so on for Supersport. The Superstock riders were exempt, as they don't make a lot of money out of riding. That was another issue that Peter raised.

'Look, you guys haven't had an increase in prize money for four years. If Chris Vermuelen rides in England and wins a 600cc race, he'll receive more prize money than he would for winning a World Supersport race. If Ben Bostrom went back home and won a domestic superbike race he'd receive more than he would for winning both World Superbike races,' said Peter.

It would appear that American race winners receive $20,000, while we receive less than £3,000. The payments for Superpole are also peanuts. Pole position receives £1,000 while second place gets just £500. Yet they want to build Superpole up as the big showcase event of the Saturday. So why not add to the spectacle by making it £10,000 for the winner? That way the punters know that every rider is going all out to set the fastest possible lap. Personally, I couldn't ride any harder than I do. But other riders must be mindful of where they stand in the championship. It would be nice to know, though, that if you've stuck your neck on the line to achieve pole position that you are being properly rewarded for it.

At least we are now speaking with one voice. Troy Corser did a good job in Australia and without him we would have had to ride on a flooded track. If that happened now, Peter would just go round to the top five riders, ask their opinion, and tell the organisers what was happening. Before this organisation was set up, if SBK wanted next year's third round to be on the Isle of Man, and the teams that we were contracted to agreed to that request, then there wouldn't have been a lot we could have done about it. That's an extreme example, but it shows that we now have a say in things.

Saturday, 1 September 2001

This morning's session was stopped for three quarters of an hour after two riders, Steve Martin and Robert Ulm crashed on oil that Marty Craggill's bike had deposited. They lost it at 140mph on the brakes, which is a big old crash, but both were okay. The delay worked out really well for me. We had changed the gearing overnight to give me a few more revs everywhere, but I soon realised that it wasn't enough. Then, on the lap on which I'd decided to come in, I saw the yellow flags while coming down the back straight and spotted the oil, just touched it and thought 'Ooh! That was a close one.' We were able to use the time taken to clear up the oil to change the gearing again to give me even more revs. Then it was just a case of getting some laps under my belt as I still felt as though I was learning the place.

We made a few small changes to the suspension and, after seven or eight laps, I was quicker than I had been on yesterday's qualifier. Then we tried the Japanese 150 tyre, that we were sure was going to be the race tyre. Other people had done more laps on it than I had and they were convinced it would be the one to use. It's also the one that I had run at Brands and Laguna, so I was getting to know it inside out despite the fact that Dunlop will change it ever so slightly depending on the track. It has brilliant side grip but not a lot of drive grip, which means that it spins controllably and doesn't 'snap'. Instead the tyre taps you gracefully on your shoulder and says 'Right, I'm going to break traction here', giving you plenty of notice. So you can almost get into a groove where you know that you would not fall off in a race because it is giving you so much feel. When I stuck a qualifier in I went from 13th to first, before dropping down to fourth by a couple of tenths. I would have settled for that last night, all I needed to be was a little bit more consistently fast, with a tad more control.

We tried a different gearing for the afternoon session, but it didn't work and we wasted the third out of four sessions here. I was riding as hard as I could but the lap times were just not there, having gone one tooth shorter to try and provide more revs so that I could use third gear instead of second in places. The result, though, was that the bike was lazy in third gear. So, just before sticking a qualifier in, we went back to the original setting and I was convinced that it was better than before. We have, however, struggled with gearing all weekend and I can't help thinking that it's been at the expense of doing laps on race tyres and also making sure the chassis is properly set up.

Still, I managed to set the second fastest time of the session on the qualifier before a sprinkling of rain fell before Superpole. That meant that a wet Superpole was declared, where you have a maximum of 12 laps in a 50 minutes period in which to set your fastest time. I went out of the garage for a good look at the weather conditions and, apart from realising that a fair few people had travelled from England to support us, decided that the weather might get worse. The track wasn't going to get any drier than it was at the start of the session, so James and I went out straight away. I couldn't understand why the others, except for Chili, didn't do the same. If there had been a quick downpour, we would have been one, two and three on the grid while they struggled in the wet. But that's one of the reasons why we are such a good team. We sit down and discuss these things and there are not too many chiefs.

The track was actually slightly greasy but I managed to do a time that was only a second short of a very good lap time which, considering I was being careful not to touch any kerbs in the wet, was pretty good. Having got that lap in the bank, and with the track still drying, I went back out and bettered that time, leaving me in first position. Then, with a few of my 12 laps remaining, it was just a case of sitting it out for a while to see what happened. With 11 minutes remaining I went out on my final qualifier but made a mistake on the first, crucial lap, by braking too late. For some unusual reason, though, you seem to be able to get two good laps out of a qualifier around this circuit. I was lucky to get a second bite at the cherry and set the fastest time for yet another pole position.

At other venues I would have gone to bed knowing that I'd be in the top three or four and battling for the lead. Here, I was not exactly over-confident. We had done no distance to speak of on race tyres and I know tomorrow is going to be a tough old day. Colin Edwards has been consistently fast, as has Ruben Xaus, but he does not generally put two good races together, so Edwards looks like the man to beat.

Before that, though, England had 11 Germans to beat in the World Cup qualifier in Munich. I'd expected a few people to be round at the motorhome wanting to watch my telly, as Suzi Perry had nipped round before the afternoon session. Her luggage had not arrived in Germany, so she needed to borrow some eyeliner from Kathryn before doing the live feed for Superpole. They were trying to plan where to watch the game, so I told them they would be welcome as long as they didn't bring the whole crew, as it might have been a bit of a squeeze. As it happened, we watched the game on our own and it was a strange feeling. If the game had been a draw until right at the end when England sneaked a win, there would have been unbelievable elation, and I felt that kind of elation when we went 2-1 up. I was also excited when we went 3-1 up. But from then on it seemed a bit of an anti-climax and the game lost its appeal.

Sunday, 2 September 2001

I must have had other things on my mind during the football last night because the 5-1 scoreline was on everyone's lips today. Suzi interviewed me for Grandstand on the pit wall to a backdrop of Union Jacks and blaring foghorns, asking what it was like to be an Englishman competing in Germany today. To be perfectly honest, it could have been anywhere in the world because race day always feels the same, regardless of what the national football team has done the night before.

It was cold for the morning warm-up and the track was slippery, so I could not tell if any of the changes that we had made had had any effect. There was no option but to stick with what we had already got for the first race. It didn't help when I got my second worst start of the year, after Phillip Island. I actually wasn't ready for the light to change. The red light is normally on for two seconds, so I don't pull the clutch in straight away because I don't want it to get too hot. By the time I did pull it in the light had gone out, so I was caught off guard. To make matters worse I had a terrible first corner. I was on the outside and my view was blocked by the rear of another bike. If the guy had grabbed his front brake, then I was in the back of him without any doubt, so I braked a little bit, to have a quick look, and three or four other riders dived through. I managed to pass a couple of them back by the end of the first lap, but was still down in 10th.

As early as lap three, by which time I'd passed James and moved up to ninth, I knew I was going to have problems because I just wasn't getting any grip. I'd been lulled into a false sense of security by the qualifying tyres that we'd used in practice. They had allowed the bike to turn whereas, on race tyres, the bike didn't want to turn in the horseshoe corners. Any of the other riders that I was with could open the throttle there and continue to turn, while my bike would want to go in a straight line. I was particularly weak in those three sections, and I could only make up a bit of ground on a couple of other corners. I would almost get back in touch, before losing three bike lengths again on the next lap at the horseshoes. It was quite mind-numbing and not enjoyable.

The best I could do was to pass Regis Laconi and Troy Corser, so there was at least some consolation from a championship point of view. I thought that I couldn't do much worse in the next race. Changes were made to the front forks to help with the steering, although Stewart didn't need to explain what he was doing – I just let him get on with it. We had no choice but to use the same tyre as the choice was between either the one I'd used in the first race, or a really bad one. You have to say that Ben Bostrom is riding well at the moment and there is no way that he could have produced consistent 1:27 laps, as race winner Colin Edwards and second placed Ruben Xaus were doing. This was definitely a Michelin track.

My start to the second race was obviously better, although

still not brilliant, and I was fifth at the end of the first lap. I was sitting behind Akira Yanagawa when I made a silly mistake and braked too late. I thought I was going to run into the back of the Kawasaki and had to pick the bike up, causing me to run wide and, just my luck, into a load of cement dust and shit on the edge of the track. That meant I lost all drive going into the straight and Bayliss, Bostrom and Gregorio Lavilla came through. It's fatal to let people through here because there are so few places to pass. I had to be content, therefore, briefly swapping places with Lavilla before Chili and Okada picked me off by lap 13.

With around six laps to go Corser passed me although I was able to get him back almost straight away. Once that happened I forgot all about the guys in front and concentrated on blocking Corser off by making myself wide down the straight so that he would have to come down the wrong side. As a result of that I dropped my lap times to 1:30s and lost all corner speed, but that didn't matter so much because there was only one line through the corners. But, to salvage anything from a terrible weekend, I had to beat him over the line. If I hadn't managed to do that, there would have been no positives to take from here.

I felt very tired after the race. The last time I had been anything like so exhausted was probably after the second race in Japan. It is a physically demanding circuit but, because the races were not going well, I was probably trying to overcompensate in places. That's when I ride tensely. And if I'm tense, I'm slow. It's when I'm not trying too hard and the riding comes naturally that I am fast. I had a 20 minutes chat with Darrell afterwards. He was obviously disappointed but it's more difficult for someone like him to understand, even though he knows so much about racing, why I was a second and a half slower than yesterday. I tried to explain that some of it was down to the set-up, although I am totally responsible because it's my job to make sure the bike is set up correctly.

Darrell pointed out that because this track is similar to Valencia, we might need to do some work on the more twisty circuits. It was good constructive criticism because it's clear they don't suit my riding style and that's something we have to address and improve on for next year. I need to alter the set-up and also maybe my riding style. So we have already talked about doing some testing during the winter so that I can do race distances on this type of horseshoe track.

I've not followed Xaus, who won the second race comfortably, in races except for Monza, which is a completely different sort of track. But I have seen him in practice and, in my opinion, he rides the bike all wrong. He is very ragged and upsets the bike with his body language. It's completely the opposite to how I ride a bike, but maybe there is something I can learn from that because I can't seem to get round this sort of track. Maybe I need to hang off a bit more. I thought he had done well to finish second in the first race so I was surprised to find out he'd won the second. I can only take my hat off to anyone who can put a race together as he did here. Ruben is not someone I speak to all that much, although he seems a very approachable and confident young man. It will be interesting to see how the win affects him. The last thing you want to see is someone getting a bit clever, although I doubt he will be like that.

Although we were talking as though next year is a 'done' deal, I have obviously not done myself any favours here. If I were a betting man, I would now say that the ideal package – me at GSE on a 2002 factory Ducati – is not going to happen. Ruben Xaus has had a very good weekend, winning the second race comfortably, so Ducati are not going to want to sack him. And, if Bostrom and Bayliss stay, they are probably not going to want to run another factory bike with GSE. After all there is only so much that Ducati can do.

Assen – round 12

Thursday, 6 September 2001

Instead of seizing the chance to have a few days break, I couldn't wait to get to Assen as soon as possible so that I could forget about what had happened last weekend. I've had a chance to think things through properly and I know that the results weren't just my fault. There were lots of different reasons. I hadn't been there before, we had concentrated on just going faster rather than working on race strategy, and I rode appallingly around the two or three corners where it was possible to pass other riders. That was about the only thing that I could have worked a lot harder on. We got everything out in the open yesterday in a two-hour meeting with Colin and Stewart.

'Whatever happened at the weekend, we need to make sure it doesn't happen again,' Colin said. 'So we need to analyse it and you need to tell me exactly what you were thinking and what you now feel about it.'

'I think we again fell into the trap of changing the bike too much, messing around with the gearing and not doing enough laps,' I suggested.

It was, as usual, all very positive although Colin did say when he hadn't seen certain things the same way. But that's how a good team should work; to meet everything head on, not brush any issues under the carpet and just hope everything will be okay by the time of the next meeting.

One of the things he focused on was which riders had made progress during races and which ones had slipped back. After such a bad start in the first race, another factor that had to be brought up, the rest of the race was quite positive in that I had moved consistently through the field to seventh. Colin was more disappointed with the second race because I had dropped from fifth to tenth.

I did get a chance to have a bit of a light-hearted dig back. I'd arrived at Oschersleben to find out that Robert Bonazzi would no longer be with the team for the rest of the season. We had been under the impression that he was a computer technician, although it turned out that he was actually a race engineer, like Stewart, and it was obvious that two people could not do the same job. We had a meeting with him earlier in the season to explain the situation, and I had heard rumours for a couple of months that he would be leaving. Basically it had been decided with Ducati, who had seconded him to us, that he was wasting his talents with our team because there was not enough for him to do. He accepted the situation and there were no hard feelings on either side.

'See what happens for the first round without Roberto,' I joked. Now that everyone had got things of their chest I could start to think positively about this weekend.

Before arriving here we drove to a campsite on the other side of Hanover from where Colin Edwards and his wife Alyssia, Ben Bostrom and Karl Muggeridge and their girlfriends, Cat and Isabelle, went rock-climbing in the constant drizzle. Kathryn and I went for some schnitzel at a local restaurant with Steve Plater, a Supersport rider, who had fallen three times at Oschersleben and was nursing a bad graze on his arm. It's the first time I'd spent much time with him and he seems like a good guy.

It was still raining the next morning and the others decided to head off. I was feeling sluggish so went for a run to clear my head, by which time the sun had come out and Colin and Ben decided to go climbing after all. We headed off on a shortcut down some A-roads and spotted a Chinese restaurant where we could stop for dinner. It was meant to be a quick 30-minute stop but I pointed to the wrong banquet and we stayed there for nearly three hours, pigging out on eight courses. It meant we didn't arrive at Assen until 11 o'clock that evening, when the gates had been locked for the night, so we had to park outside, which I didn't have a problem with because I know that rules are rules.

After the meeting with Colin and Stewart yesterday I went into Assen with Kathryn to have a look around. You can become fed up of just hanging around the paddock, so it was nice to have a change of scenery although there's not a lot to see except for shops. I had to ask before leaving for the town, whether the coffee shops that you find in Amsterdam, which sell drugs legally over the counter, were found in this part of the country. But I can assure you that the one we went into only sold cappuccino. I have actually been disappointed that I haven't been drug tested this year, and as far as I know none of the other riders have been, although there is always the threat of a random test. I'm 99.9 per cent certain that none of the riders are on anything but, if somebody was, the lack of testing is a loophole that can be exploited. Bearing in mind that last year's championship was virtually decided on that subject, when Noriyuki Haga had points deducted after testing positive for ephedrine in South Africa, the officials' stance is even more surprising. I can't help but feel that they were so embarrassed by that saga that they have been willing to turn a blind eye to it this year.

I also managed to find time today to kick a football around with James and his mechanic Skip Warnock. I love Skip – real name Anthony – to bits. He gets a hard time from everybody because he is small and an Aussie - hence the name Skip (as in Skippy the bush kangaroo) – but he gives as good as he gets. I also feel like I've got a lot in common with him and am on his wavelength. That's not just because he's into motocrossing and BMX, but he also has a really dry sense of humour. I'm not sure about his football, though. I used to be okay as a kid and- - surprise, surprise – my mum thinks I could have been a professional!

By now I was starting to get focused on the weekend by walking the track with Stewart. I'm not 100 per cent sure going into this round whether the circuit suits me or not, as I've never had a good result here. It's like no other track, in that the corners flow into each other so smoothly and are so banked that you can't believe how fast you can run into them. But the weather is always mixed, at best.

Fogarty obviously had some special affinity with the track here and, whatever it was, it was awesome. Maybe he won on his first outing, so that every time he came back he was buzzing and knew he was going to win. A record of 12 wins out of 16 races speaks for itself. He knew how to attack the circuit by carrying corner speed and hanging off the bike, a bit like Xaus does now. The other thing to bear in mind is that it's a difficult circuit to get dialled into because the laps are so much longer than normal, meaning that you can't do as many in any one session. More laps means more experience and more data so, with fewer laps, you often find yourself guessing about set-up.

Friday, 7 September 2001

The weather has been terrible here all week. We are, after all, right next door to England in the north of Holland, so what do you expect? And this morning was no different. I managed just two laps before it started to rain around the back of the track, so I came back in until the weather cleared up. After another seven or eight laps I came in again to try a different tyre and was fastest at that point but, almost as soon as I went back out, it started to rain again. When I arrived back at the garage I was back down to third, and we waited for a few minutes to see what the weather was going to do. It started to bucket down, so we then set the bike up for wet weather conditions. This can sometimes only take around five minutes but there was a bit more to do than normal so it actually lasted for 15 minutes and I only squeezed in another five minutes on the track. It was enough for just one flying lap, although the gearing change that we had spent so long on for the wet felt really good. The time had therefore been well spent because, if we have more wet conditions, we know that the gearing is sorted out.

The weather cleared up for the afternoon qualifying session and I was on it straight away. There had been nothing to change from the few dry laps of the morning but we were already struggling to find a tyre that didn't start spinning after something like three laps. They were spinning controllably, not violently, but it was still not ideal. After half an hour we were on our third choice. But there was a more pressing problem. The bike had been jumping out of gear.

'I think the gearbox is about to go,' I told the team. Everybody just looked blankly at me, because we had not had one go all year and there was nothing anyone could do.

'What do you want to do?' said Colin, knowing that the other bike was set for wet conditions. Even so, we might still not have changed bikes because it only seemed as though the gearbox was going to go and these things are difficult to predict accurately.

'Well, I suppose we'll just have to carry on,' I said.

The fourth tyre felt really good and I was just starting to get into my swing when I came out of one of the corners in second gear and went to move up into third. It felt like the bike, however, went straight into fourth.

'Oh no! What's happening here,' I thought before there was an awful noise and the back wheel momentarily locked up, so I grabbed the clutch straight away and coasted off the track.

I was desperate to get back to the garage as quickly as possible but the breakdown people wanted to put the bike on the back of the truck which was giving me a lift back.

'No, forget the bike. Just get me back, will you?' I pleaded to the driver, who was sitting there smoking a big cigar while I sweating buckets and puffing and panting. I only had two choices – to play by his rules or to walk all the way back, which is a fair distance at Assen.

When I eventually arrived back there was no more than 18 minutes remaining.

'Try the standard harder 587 English tyre,' Colin said.

'That won't work, I can tell you that now. Are we not wasting our time with that?' I said.

'Try it anyway, as we need to know for sure,' he insisted, because although the team had thought that softer tyres would have been right for this track, throughout the day we'd been moving towards harder and harder compounds.

I actually did go faster than I had done on the other race tyres I'd tried, but more through riding harder than from any extra grip it provided. It was actually terrible, so I was relieved to stick a qualifier in. My first lap was not good, therefore I had no choice but to try and get another fast lap out of the tyre. That's like trying to get three laps out of a qualifier on any other circuit, because Assen is such a long track. I was spinning a lot and I classed that lap as though it was done on race rubber, because the qualifier certainly wasn't hooking up. I didn't feel in too bad a shape with the seventh fastest time, of 2:04.407, although Xaus had gone really quick again with a time of 2:02.409, almost two seconds quicker than me and 0.8 seconds faster than Corser in second.

Michelin might well have found a new tyre that better suits Xaus's style, but I tend not to believe paddock rumours. I know things that have been said about me in the past that have been bullshit. And who cares, anyway? It's all about journalists needing to fill their magazines and there are so many on the market at the moment in England that there's a lot of space to fill with such tittle-tattle. If you ask me, the fact that Xaus is riding so much better is probably more to do with the fact that his job with Ducati was on the line unless he pulled his finger out for the final few rounds.

Kathryn took the train from Assen to Amsterdam to fly back home to be bridesmaid at the wedding of two of our really good friends, Zoe and Andy, which I was disappointed to miss. However, I don't think I'd have got very far if I'd asked for the weekend off! It meant, though, that I was bored rigid by my own company after the team went back to their hotel. I watched a film called The Bachelor – which was awful – and thank goodness I'm not a bachelor. I don't mind my own company now and again but if I had the choice between Kathryn being here and not being here, I'd have her with me a million times over.

Saturday, 8 September 2001

After analysing the telemetry last night we decided to change the gearing to give me less revs everywhere, so that I could carry more corner speed. It had been wet for the Supersport qualifying which took place before us, but the track was drying throughout that hour, so I went out on slicks in order to test the new gearing before it started to rain on lap two. Even at this early stage I have never known a weekend like it for switching between wet and dry conditions. All I could do was to ride round on full wets, although I was able to get into a bit of a rhythm at last. I could at least build up my lap times as the session progressed, although I was only really finding my feet and I ended up seventh fastest. The bike felt very good and, after we changed the gearing to the wet setting, it was even better.

All things considered it wasn't a bad session. I am good in the wet in a race situation but in practice I tend to err on the side of caution – probably a bit too much. But you are who you are and that's the way I ride in the wet, with everything on the safe side. Some riders throw caution to the wind but I prefer to build my confidence, find the limit and find my breaking points. It's a bit stupid riding flat out before the actual race – the only thing that will happen is you will scare yourself or crash and lose all your confidence. All in all, I would probably be fairly happy if tomorrow's races were run in wet conditions.

Superpole warm-up in the afternoon was dry for six or seven laps, so at least I finally got a chance to test the new gearing. I was actually second fastest in the session behind Bostrom, in dry conditions. But we already know that we will not be able to beat a Michelin rider who has the right set-up, as we still haven't found a tyre that lasts for more than two laps without spinning. Goodness knows what we are going to run tomorrow if the races are dry because we know we are going to speedway everywhere on all the tyres that we've tested. Again, Xaus looks to be the one with a good package around here. Realistically, my goal is to try and be the best Dunlop finisher tomorrow.

Another handicap was the intense pain I was feeling in my right arm. I have had this problem before and the first time I felt it was at Assen in 1995, when I riding a 500cc. The series doctor, Claudio Costa, told me that it was just a bit of tendonitis and that there was nothing I could do except to have massages and take painkillers. Apparently Loris Capirossi suffers from it a lot. With me it comes and goes and I felt it a little bit in Germany, although it disappeared after taking some Aspirin. First thing yesterday morning, however, it was back. This circuit does not help because the straights are not true straights, but contain little kinks. So you are constantly pushing and pulling with your arms. Strangely, considering I'm left handed, I seem to do a lot of work with my right hand.

The pain is actually underneath the biceps and around the triceps on my upper arm, so it is nothing to do with muscle pump in the forearm. It does not actually cause much of a problem when I am riding but there is immense pain when I stop. On my slowing down lap, when I have stopped concentrating on the track, I become much more aware of it. By the time I am entering the pits I can hardly clench my fists.

The agony can almost make you cry and last year at Cadwell Park, when I was in Charlie's clinic, there was another rider called Steve McMillan who was also suffering from the same thing. He is a big, hard, strong lad but he was almost in tears. The problem is that it is not a visible thing like a pumped up muscle, so it's difficult for people to appreciate the pain. When it started to rain during the afternoon session I went straight to see the doctors and they gave me a rub down.

'It's because it's so cold,' said one of the *Clinica Mobile* doctors, although I knew that the temperature was nothing to do with it because I have also suffered in hot climates.

I know that it won't be a problem for tomorrow's races

because I can take painkillers and have massage to get through it. However, if it is really bad after the first race then I'll have some painkilling injections and I know the pain will disappear altogether, although I'll get a delayed reaction on Monday and it won't be any fun driving my motorhome back to England. Thankfully, it's the end of the season and I have all winter to recover. The pain is not going to be my main problem tomorrow – starting from the fourth row of the grid is!

Superpole was a lottery. The track was wet, but not saturated, and a wet Superpole was declared. So, as in Germany, I went out straight away in case conditions didn't improve. I did four laps and recorded a decent time before coming in to see how things were panning out. The track seemed to be drying so I went out again with a wet front tyre and an intermediate rear. On that first lap I realised that the track was now dry enough for slicks. On my first lap out on slicks I was 0.6 seconds up on the first split, and heading for another pole position, when the heavens absolutely opened. I had to abort the lap and, because it had rained so hard, there was no way I was going to be able to improve my time. I had missed the short window when the track conditions were at their best. The trouble was that 14 other riders hadn't!

If I'd stayed on the track with the wet front and intermediate rear I would probably have been starting from the second row and not the fourth. But I wanted to be on pole again, and having studied the clouds, I was sure that I would have time for the changeover to slicks. As it turned out I was less than a minute out from being able to do a dry lap.

Even though the track was now saturated I went back out on wets towards the end of the session, knowing that I only had to improve my time by a second in order to move up a row. It wasn't feasible, but the crowd seemed to appreciate my efforts. I have been in this situation before, when you feel that you can't do a certain time, only to go out and achieve it, so it was certainly worth the risk. It also gave me a chance to push myself to the limit in the wet, in case it rains again tomorrow.

I have probably not sat this far back on a grid since I was riding for Kawasaki in 1998, and I can't even remember an instance in that year when I was as low as 15th. I started from the back of the grid at Oulton Park last year, but that was because I stalled the bike on the line. All I can hope for is to get a flyer and have a good first corner. I have to bear in mind that, having started from pole at Oschersleben, I was down in tenth at the first corner. The aim is therefore to try and be tenth coming out of the first corner here.

It's certainly not the end of the world, especially at this circuit which has a few half-decent straights where you can pick a couple of riders off in one move, if they have punched a big enough hole in the air for you. It's actually quite weird because I feel almost jubilant and very relaxed. I know that I have good set-ups for the wet and dry – at least for a Dunlop rider. If I were on pole, however, I would have been thinking 'I'm sure to be picked off by a Michelin rider'. Now, I have absolutely nothing to lose, unless Lucio Pedercini decides to pull his finger out and I end up 16th!

Fogarty popped round to my motorhome for a brief chat in the evening with his wife Michaela, whom I'd not seen much this season. It was nice just to have a bit of company for a while.

Sunday, 9 September 2001

The track was bone dry in some places and damp in others for the warm-up this morning. So, as well as practising a few starts, the team also practised a tyre change in case the conditions altered suddenly during the race. It went really well and after that, I strung together as many laps as I have done all weekend here. We still hadn't chosen a dry tyre for the race, though. This might sound really strange, but I never did find out what tyre we actually decided on for the races.

'I know that none of the tyres work, so just speak to Dunlop and you decide,' I told Stewart before the first race when it was clear that we would have to run slicks.

Thankfully my start was as good as I could have hoped for but I ruined that good work by having crap first and second corners when I took them in first gear instead of second. I made my way up to ninth by the end of the first lap and the rest of the race was totally enjoyable, as I was always moving up through the field. I took James on lap three, Okada the following lap, and then Corser and Yanagawa on the sixth lap to leave me in fifth, but some way behind Chili. The Kawasakis and Hondas did appear fast but I could stay in their slipstream so there was no problem because I knew I could have them on the brakes. I just had one big moment going through the final chicane – and it nearly had me off. I got my timing all wrong and, as I was changing direction, the bike bucked and weaved and kicked me in the face. I was furious at myself but, when the rain eventually arrived, with three laps remaining, I was still in fifth. I wasn't going to catch Chili and Corser was closing in on me, so the shortened race was a bit of a blessing. Corser's bike is a bit faster than mine so he could have passed me on the straight, although I would have fancied my chances of getting him back through the chicane, where I was pretty good. Apart from that obvious reason, I was glad that the race was stopped straight away because sometimes they can wait half a lap by which time three people have crashed, and there's always a chance that it could be you. Bayliss did his title chances no harm by finishing ahead of

Colin Edwards, who was third, although Xaus made the point that he was following team orders by overtaking his Ducati team-mate just before the end, before allowing Troy back through almost immediately.

It was obviously very disappointing for the huge British following that I'd qualified on the fourth row, and the build-up to the second race was quite eerie. Suzi Perry was live on Grandstand, going through the grid, with the claxons going mad in the stands, although the kind of fans that travel from Britain to Assen do seem to get behind all the riders and are not as partisan as somewhere like Brands. My best section of the track, though, was going into the last corner where the majority of the Brits were situated, so I could feel their support during the races.

We had put three extra clicks of rebound damping on the rear shock for the second race, to give the bike more control when it was sliding. In the first race, the rear wheel had been kicking back quite violently so we needed to slow it down. We also changed the rear tyre for the second race because, as predicted, the first one had not been good. I think the Michelin riders were even struggling, although their tyres were hooking up better on the faster corners. When I was behind Yanagawa, though, I could see that he was having some problems, albeit on the opposite lock. As soon as I started to lift my knee off the road and accelerated coming out of corners the wheel started to spin. The more I turned the throttle, the more it spun. It's a bit like a car at a traffic lights: once the tyre has started to spin, the more you put your foot down the more violently the wheel is going to spin and you end up going nowhere. So I was keeping the bike on half-throttle until the tyre bit, before then opening it a bit more. You almost feel like you are not trying in that situation, as it's weird to have to close the gas off almost immediately after opening it.

After another good start I was tenth again at the end of the first lap, passed Regis Laconi on the next and Bostrom on the third. I've no idea what happened to Bostrom this weekend. It's possible that the track just does not suit him because he likes to slide the bike into corners so much, whereas this track is more about carrying corner speed. After passing James on the fourth lap I was behind Yanagawa again and had a good dice with him for the rest of the race. After four laps behind him, I moved into fifth again for another four laps, before he got me back on the 13th. But I was really good on the final fast left-hander and could make up about ten bike lengths on him through that section, knowing I could pass him at the chicane.

'Should I wait until the last lap to attack him,' I thought. But you can actually think about it too much and, in the past, I have missed opportunities to pass people by leaving it too late. Something might happen, like having a slide on the last lap, and your chance has gone. So I took him on the very next lap and managed to hold him off for the final two to finish fifth again. This time Corser had finished third, again behind Bayliss and Xaus, so he actually gained a few points on me in the championship over the weekend, although his fourth place is still in my sights for Imola.

The slightly more significant development, as far as the championship was concerned, was Colin Edwards finishing tenth. With Troy winning the second race it meant that Edwards was 52 points behind with only 50 up for grabs in Italy, so Troy was the new world champion. I'm really pleased for him. They say that good guys don't normally win, but his success proves otherwise. He was British champion as my team-mate just two years ago, so I only feel like I'm a year behind him. If I get a better bike next year, there is no genuine reason to say that I can't win the world championship. It's a dream, but I am not just saying that because it might be what people want to hear. I genuinely do believe that.

I tried to do a five-minute burn-out to give the British fans something to cheer after the race. I stopped short of doing a rolling burn-out because I have seen them go horribly wrong for riders like Jamie Robinson, who once high-sided doing this and could have hurt himself very badly. I was in full flow when I heard a loud bang – the tyre had popped. I had to make my way back to the garage, hoping that that short distance wouldn't wreck the wheel. This sequence of failed celebrations was becoming a bit embarrassing.

And that wasn't my only embarrassing celebration after racing at Assen. We used to return home on the ferry on Sunday night after the races and in 1997 I was sharing a cabin with Fogarty. I was completely ratted – while he was completely ratty. He was in the foulest mood possible. He had actually won the race but was in his bunk complaining about a pain in his chest. It might have been a torn muscle between his ribs but he has the skinniest body going, so I couldn't believe he had any muscles to pull.

'You are going to have to get the captain to get me some painkillers,' he moaned, as I sneaked back into the cabin with a girl that I had got friendly with in my drunken state. Needless to say this was long before I'd met Kathryn, and on this occasion it was any port in a storm, if you'll excuse the shipping pun.

'Shhhhuddup you puff,' I slurred back at him, although I was aware that he was trying to watch my drunken fumblings on the next bed. There wasn't much to see, though, because I'd had way too much to drink and it just wasn't happening, so it wasn't long before the girl gave up and rejoined the party.

This year's trip home was not quite as eventful. I had promised to turn up at a track day that my brother, Carl, was attending at Donington on Tuesday. It was his first time round there and he wanted a bit of help with lines around the track and I didn't want to let him down. So I set off from the paddock at 8pm to get the overnight ferry from Calais. It was a lonely old drive and I had time to reflect on just how much I have missed Kathryn this weekend. During the day I am always busy, but she helps me to switch off from racing at night in the motorhome. Without her my mind is literally racing until the moment I fall asleep. Even with the telly on I'll be thinking about gearing or set-up. Then I might put a bike video on and start thinking 'What did Fogarty do around here?' That can wear you out because there is no time for your body to have a rest, so I perhaps did not realise until now how important it is to have Kathryn around.

Imola – round 13

Thursday, 27 September 2001

It's been a pretty momentous couple of weeks – a time that puts racing and sport in general into perspective. I was at Silverstone on the morning of Tuesday, 11 September, taking a written exam that I needed to pass for a car race I'm doing on October 7. One of my sponsors, Ross from Travelworld, races Global Lights – single seater cars containing a motorcycle engine but without an open wheel. They have a guest slot for their race at Cadwell next weekend, so I decided to accept the offer of the drive for a bit of public relations as well as a bit of fun. I came out of the exam to find a lot of people standing around in a reception room, all glued to the television. I didn't bother to find out what they were watching and made my way out when my mobile rang.

'Neil, have you seen the news? Two planes have crashed into the World Trade Centre,' gasped Kathryn.

I glanced back at the television, but couldn't really make out what was happening so I went back to the car and switched the radio on, although I didn't really need to because Kathryn called me every two minutes with updates. It was sounding more and more serious with every call.

Nevertheless, I carried on towards Donington, to see how my brother had done at his track day. From there I drove to Manchester

Airport, as I still hadn't been home since Assen. I met Kathryn there and she was in quite a state about it all. It wasn't until we got home, and I saw the pictures of the buildings collapsing, that it started to sink in. Dangerous sports like mine aren't everyone's cup of tea but this kind of thing just goes to show how vulnerable we all are.

Kathryn was on stand-by to fly just a few days later, but was not expecting to have to travel. On the Saturday morning, at the last minute, she was told she had to go to Orlando. A few hours later, I received another call, this time from her on the plane, telling me that she had actually been put on a flight to New York's Newark airport – one of the first allowed back into the city. I wasn't at all pleased, and her dad felt the same way, but she was pretty blasé.

'It's the safest place to fly to at the moment,' she insisted. It was probably very true but that's not a lot of comfort for the people at home, stuck with all the horrendous images.

Her summary of the experience on her return was that the city was strangely 'nice' for once. It's probably not what you would expect someone to say, but I could understand what she meant. New York can be a cold place for strangers, but Kathryn found it really uplifting to see how everyone had pulled together behind the Stars and Stripes and how friendly people had become. She was not able to get too close to the actual scene, but still felt as though she was caught up in a film set. The one thing she found particularly upsetting was to see someone putting posters up, appealing for help in finding his missing son.

When I was asked, a few days later by my local paper, whether the final round at Imola should go ahead, I almost laughed. There are two Americans in the World Superbike series, Ben Bostrom and Colin Edwards, and I'm sure that they would have wanted to continue riding. It wouldn't really have achieved anything if we hadn't competed here, except for showing that the terrorists could indeed bring everything to a halt.

Set against the backdrop of events in America, my own big news that week was put into perspective. but it obviously did not seem that way to me. I had been offered a deal by GSE at the start of the week and I'd been told that Ducati wanted to make us their official factory World Superbike team for 2003 and 2004, when they go GP racing. Until then, we would continue as we had done for this year on one-year-old machinery. I was not ecstatic about that, I have to say. However, I have been assured that the new factory bikes might only have an additional two or three horsepower next year, whereas I should have an extra ten from this year's bike. We are also hoping to get hold of the engine as soon as possible, to try and get a bit more out of it. Ducati have also promised to pass down any new engine developments.

The other areas of concern that Roger and I had about the offer were the choice of leathers and tyres, as well as a slight issue over the money that had been offered by GSE. Ducati wanted me to wear Dianese leathers in 2003, but I enjoy wearing Axo and have built up a good relationship with them. They ideally wanted me to run on Michelin tyres but it was agreed that it would be in the team's interests for me to continue on Dunlops. It was all very positive but we wanted a few of those grey areas cleared up before we signed anything and we agreed to talk again to Darrell later in the week when, hopefully, he would have some answers.

In the meantime, Roger met up with Castrol Honda boss Neil Tuxworth, to explain the situation. They also offered me a deal, but it was probably not as good as we thought it might be. The fact that I wanted to stay with GSE so badly meant that Honda would had to have offered me something unbelievable in order for me to even contemplate leaving. Again, money was not the biggest issue as they could have matched the GSE deal. It was the fact that there was only a one-year deal on the table, for a different team, on a different bike and on different tyres. I would have wanted the security of a fall-back plan because of that in case things didn't go well in the first season. They were not prepared to offer me that second year, though. I wasn't at the meeting, and can only go by what Roger told me, but it seemed that my role would have been very much as a number two rider to Colin Edwards. At this point in my career, I need to go into a new team as number one, or at least as another rider's equal. There's no point being stuck in the corner of the garage looking after myself – I have been there and done that as a young lad. In a way, I was pleased because it made my decision even easier.

Roger rang me on Wednesday night, after Darrell had come back to him with a slightly improved financial package, and said:

'We have got answers for everything we needed to know and it's everything we wanted to hear. The deal is there – it's up to you. You don't want to mess anyone about because these people are your friends now.'

We had met them halfway on a few things, such as the financial package. That's always the case with these things, and I am really happy with what I am being paid. The choice of leathers is still a grey area, although I wasn't going to dig my heels in over that, and I was happy that James was being retained as my team-mate. Hopefully he will be a better rider and maybe we can start to help each other, as this year it has pretty much been one-way traffic. I don't want a pat on the back for that although the bottom line is that you have to bat for yourself.

The new contract was, though, a load off my mind and I was able to enjoy a great Gold Cup weekend at Oliver's Mount in Scarborough the following weekend. Jamie Whitham was doing some parade laps and people such as Barry Sheene and Steve Parrish were also appearing, so I jumped at the chance to do some ride rounds for the spectators as well. It was a good chance to meet up with people I'd raced against in 1991 and 1992, like

Chris Palmer and Alan Patterson, who's a mad Irishman who has retired three or four times. He once had a bad crash at Scarborough, which is a dangerous circuit, and was in hospital for three months with a badly damaged back. We had a night out on Saturday with his mates, including a guy nicknamed Casper because he was the palest human being ever seen. He looked like he had been dragged from his own coffin for the night out. Alan didn't look a lot better the next morning, although he was more green than white. While I was getting out of my leathers after my parade laps, he was trying to find his gear, still drunk from the night before and having had a few hairs of the dog. He found one tatty red Alpinestar boot and started shouting at his mates when he couldn't find the other. In the end he had to borrow a brand new shiny blue boot, three sizes too small. His glove had a patch of leather missing three inches square.

You can't ride in those gloves,' I said. 'Why don't you put some new ones on?'

'They're comfortable!' he replied.

'But if you crash, you'll have no hand left.'

'I'm not going to crash,' he assured me. And you can't argue with that!

It was a shame for the fans that the racing had to be abandoned for three hours, after oil was spilt on the track. But the highlight of the weekend for me came from Sheene. He was riding the 500 Cagiva that John Kocinski rode in 1994 and, rumour has it, he was still trying to change the suspension despite the fact that he was 17 seconds off the pace!

Jamie Whitham was supposed to have been on a big night out with Fogarty in Manchester on the Friday night. But he'd had a call in the afternoon, to say that Carl had broken his tibia and fibula while practising for a Supermotard race which was being held in Belgium next month.

'You know what he's like,' Jamie told me. 'He wasn't prepared to go to the race, ride round, and earn himself £5,000. He will have wanted to win it and would have been pushing too hard – the daft ****!'

I'd been asked to ride in the same race by CCM. I told them I wasn't interested because those are the places where you can end your career, and if I'd suffered a similar injury, even at that time of the year, it might have affected next year's plans. Those events attract thrill-seekers – people who want to turn around and say 'I beat you, so road racing can't be that difficult,' and it is a bit rough and ready. I did feel sorry for him, though, because you can do without breaking your tib and fib at his age. Again, though, these things have to be put into perspective. I was just about to go racing at the track where Ayrton Senna lost his life in 1994.

I arrived at Imola late on Wednesday night, having decided to fly instead of driving here in the motorhome. Malcolm had brought it down, and it was all clean and levelled when we arrived and it's nice to know I don't have to drive all the way home on Monday – with a probable hangover. There was an open paddock today, which involved a lot of autograph signing for the punters before another riders' meeting. I turned up very briefly, before they got stuck into the issue of prize money again, because I didn't want to miss the chance to walk the track with Stewart and James. It's what I call a proper race track and one I should enjoy riding round. At least it's not another boring horseshoe circuit like Valencia or Oschersleben. I was surprised, however, by how bumpy the surface was. It felt uneven on a scooter, so you could imagine just how bumpy it was going to be on a race bike. It looks as though it hasn't been resurfaced for around 20 years, although parts have been patched up, and the wear and tear probably has been made worse by Formula One racing.

Friday, 29 September 2001

The plan was to just ride round as much as possible and not change the bike. The base setting we were using was similar to Assen and I tried three different tyres in the morning, when I did 25 laps, three more than any other rider and getting faster all the time. We were tending towards softer tyres, as the grip was not too good at all and we were struggling to find any tyre that didn't start to drift after just a couple of laps. I was playing catch-up again, as all the other factory teams had been here for a two-day test after Laguna Seca.

The fact that I had never been here before at all was making things doubly difficult. As a new team, the logistical difficulties of coming here during August would have been too great, especially considering that the priority was to have everything ready for Brands Hatch. I could totally understand that decision, although it will have to be different next year if we are to have a chance of winning the world championship. However, we will have more resources next year. Half of the budget is already in place and even if Darrell is unable to find a title sponsor again, he's agreed to underwrite it for another year. They seem pretty confident that another sponsor has been found, but I've heard that before!

It didn't help that I was 20 minutes late going out for the afternoon session. The team were putting a new engine into one bike and were probably only running behind by a couple of minutes. When they fired it up on the stand, it was clear there was a problem. Colin was not confident enough to let me go out with it, which was the right decision. So I had to use the other bike, on which they were changing the gearing and were having some problems with the chain. The time dragged on and on, which was really frustrating, especially at the start of the session when you are testing race tyres and not just throwing in qualifiers. Every minute that passed was a minute that I wasn't going to get back and every minute is important at this level –

especially when you haven't been to a track before. I want to be the best in the world around every track, not just fast around every track. So I wasn't happy, but managed to remain calm.

Whenever I have lost my temper with the team in previous seasons – it might have been over taking too long to change a back wheel – it has only resulted in a massive fall-out with Colin. The fact that there has not been one incident all this year tells me that the team has improved more than I've changed my approach. Shouting does not achieve anything. It's not the way to speak to people who are trying to help you.

We did change the gearing slightly, which helped to give the tyre an easier time. At the moment I'm going round four corners in first gear, and that really abuses the tyre. Ideally, I want to be doing at least three of them in second, so tomorrow morning we are going to change the gearing radically on one bike and leave it on the other. We also need to alter the suspension to try and find more grip at the rear, as I have been going speedway both into and out of the corners. Grip is everything to me because, if the bike hooks up, my lap times plummet. At the moment, though, when I turn the throttle, it's as if I'm riding on the gravel.

Before dinner I had an interview with Esquire magazine, which went as well as an interview with a reporter who knows nothing about the sport could do. That wasn't her fault, though, and she probably didn't know much about football, either, and it is nice on occasions to do press interviews when you are not preaching to the converted. But she did ask the standard two silly questions: 'How much do you earn and are there any groupies?'

Saturday, 29 September 2001

I was surprised to be called back into the garage after doing only three laps this morning.

'Your first three laps have been deleted because you were cutting across the chicane,' Colin said.

'But I was doing that yesterday as well,' I said.

'Yeah, we know, but they have decided to put a stop to it today. We didn't know anything about it, either,' he added.

It seems that Troy Corser, who hadn't had a great first day, had brought the officials attention to what was happening. He told the press last night: 'We've seen here that you get the fastest time by cutting the chicane – the difference is enormous. Now we'll see with the race director if this is going to be the solution for the next two days.'

I think that 95 per cent of the riders had been doing it yesterday and it really made no difference to me. In fact it's probably dangerous, because the bike becomes airborne for a split second. Cars always ride the kerbs but bikes normally have to stay on the tarmac, but the kerbs are so low here that we could get away with it. What it did mean, though, was that everyone had to relearn the corner this morning and while first splits were often up on yesterday's, the second split was obviously slower. We were actually having to brake a lot later, because we were going further into the track for the new line through the chicane.

Both the suspension and the gearing were better after the changes that we'd made overnight, and I went about half a second quicker on race tyres. Then I tried the Japanese tyre and decided that I was going to use it tomorrow. I already know that most of the other Dunlop riders will be going with the English one, but I am three or four tenths faster on the Japanese than I am on the English, so I have to go with what's best for me. Bostrom might have gone faster on the English tyre, but it obviously didn't suit my bike or set-up. By the end of the session I was nine tenths up on yesterday's best time on race rubber, although I didn't better yesterday's times on qualifiers. Overall, though, it was a very positive morning.

The afternoon was a different kettle of fish, and I felt as though I'd got into a rut. I couldn't even match my times from the morning. It was probably as a result of changing the offset, to try and make it easier to change direction, as well as putting stiffer springs in the front forks, in an attempt to make the bike more compliant over the bumps. All in all, though, I think I lost a bit of feeling from the bike. Even my final couple of laps on a qualifier were nothing spectacular, so I was feeling a bit demoralised before Superpole and mad with myself that I couldn't get inch perfect everywhere. It is hard work, though, trying to go faster on a track that you are still not 100 per cent confident on or comfortable with.

My Superpole lap was better than I'd done all weekend, and that is always the first aim, but I felt as though I hadn't attacked the lap properly. I was pushing hard in places, yet in others I should have let the brake off and pushed a bit more. That's what happens when you feel that you are riding on the edge and don't want to go over it. I qualified in seventh, and was happy enough to be on the second row. Going into Superpole I realised that I would have had to produce a really flukey one-off lap to make it onto the front row.

The fact that Corser had qualified on pole didn't bother me too much. While I am totally determined to finish fourth in the championship by pulling back the 10 points he has on me before tomorrow's races, I've seen him qualify well a few times and then not do anything special in the races.

Suzi Perry came round to the motorhome to do an interview for tomorrow's Grandstand with James and I in the evening. It was about the first time that we'd managed to keep a straight face when we've done joint interviews with her. In Japan she'd asked me if we were sharing information.

'Yeah, we share everything now,' I replied, with just a hint of sexual innuendo that made us all burst out laughing like teenagers. On another occasion she'd said to James that things were on the 'up and up' – with the same reaction. But we've got to remember that James is only 20 and probably goes to bed dreaming about things like that!

My mood improved enormously when I got a call confirming that John Jones of HM Plant had agreed to become title sponsors for the next three years. This is fantastic news for the whole team, and Darrell in particular.

Sunday, 30 September 2001

The Halifax Mob has been out in force again here. I can't believe that they have travelled so far yet again. If anything, they were even more mental this weekend than they have been in the past, dancing all day long to Madness on their sound system – occasionally breaking off for a chorus of 'Hodgson, Hodgson'. You appreciate support like that even more when things aren't quite going to plan, as they hadn't done so far on this round, because you can carry yourself through a weekend without support when things are going well.

The warm-up was damp, so we didn't bother to make any changes to the set-up that we'd finished with yesterday and I was content to just ride around. They were the kind of conditions when you can just touch a white line, go over the handlebars and break your wrist, and before the final races of the season, I didn't want to take that risk.

My start for the first race was as good as I could have expected and I was in the first four after the first couple of corners. I felt reasonably comfortable on the opening lap and was surprised at how quickly Xaus came past me on the straight on the second lap, especially as I'd been fast through the previous corner. The plan at that stage was to tuck in, because I knew he'd be going straight to the front. However, going flat out in fourth gear into the fast kink before the final chicane, I hit the brakes just when I closed the throttle. As soon as I did that the front folded and I lost traction. It happened so quickly that I thought I'd crashed so I let the brake off and, luckily, the bike picked itself back up, but I was now approaching the corner 30mph too fast and there was no chance of making it round. Thankfully there was a slip-road down into the pit-lane ahead. If that had not been there I would have been straight into the gravel and crashed, so I went down the pit-lane but then decided to do a U-turn rather than go straight on to the bottom, because the officials might have given me a Stop-Go penalty. The U-turn took forever and I ended up rejoining the race in last place.

It was depressing because I knew the race was over. Even if I broke the lap record on every lap thereafter I knew the best I could finish in was around tenth. So it took a few laps for me to get my frame of mind back into riding the bike and out of the doldrums. I then got my head down, although the bike didn't feel good and I realised I'd made the wrong choice of tyre with the Japanese. It was very poor by midway through the race, with very little side grip.

It was strange to pass people that you do not normally have to pass and to have a chance to study how they ride. I came up behind Giovanni Bussei at one point and thought 'Come on, get out of my way!' But he brakes really late, maybe later than anyone I have ever ridden against. Then he stops dead in the corner – that's why he is so slow – before accelerating away again. The fact that he keeps his hand on the brake for so long makes him very difficult to pass.

I had gained a few places on the final lap when Troy Bayliss and Regis Laconi were involved in a spectacular and nasty crash. I saw the replay this evening and it's when people become tangled up in their bikes that there can be serious injuries. Troy broke his collarbone. He's far from happy about it, but he'll have recovered in three weeks, so it could have been a lot worse. James also had a heavy fall on the final lap. I went to see him shivering in the medical centre and he didn't look good. He had been ill all weekend anyway, so they took him to the hospital for some checks, fearing it might be pneumonia, where it was also discovered that he was low on blood oxygen levels.

So at the end of race one I had finished in tenth place and it was a measure of how fed up I was that I didn't even bother to look at the sheet and thought I'd been 11th, one place behind Lucio Pedercini. That'll teach me to challenge him to pull his finger out at Assen.

It was obvious I needed to change my rear tyre for the second race, to the English Dunlop, and I also changed the gearing and suspension slightly. The initial race had been my first chance to string a lot of laps together around here and I realised that I needed more revs everywhere so that I could run second gear instead of first around a lot of the corners. We had gone in that direction early in the weekend, but when the tyres went off I could no longer carry second gear. As far as the suspension was concerned I needed to stop the bike backing in so much.

'I think we should keep it the same as the first race. It's better the devil you know,' said Colin.

'Let me hang myself on this one. I know what the setting was like before and there's no way I'd be able to run in the top five. If it goes wrong, it's totally my responsibility,' I insisted.

The gearing change allowed me to use second when the tyre had gone and I was more consistent – but consistently slow! And it was going slightly wrong, though nothing major until I made another small mistake, which again caused me to run off the track. Steve Martin had out-braked two or three people and when he came past me he looked as though he was going to run wide. However, he must have braked really deep in the corner and I was going to ram him so I sat it up and about five or six people came through. I lost a lot of time but it really woke me up. That's not how it should be, although I did go faster in the next part of the race than at any other time. The problem was my bike was always poor coming out of the slower corners and it was really difficult to hold my own nearer the front. It must have been more to do with the setting than the bike because, although I have lacked acceleration on other occasions, it was never as bad as this. This was not how I like to ride a motorcycle.

It is difficult to describe what I'm feeling when I'm riding. When I push really hard and catch someone I feel good. If I don't catch them I feel shit. To push, I focus a bit more, brake a bit later and turn the throttle earlier. If I eased off from the limit just two tenths of a second per lap I'd be able to ride like that all day – I'd feel like I'd never fall off. But that extra two tenths is so hard. That's the limit. If you come back from it, it's easy. But you don't win.

The team had always praised me for being kind to the bike, whereas Troy Bayliss was a butcher two years ago! He didn't use the clutch on down-changes but stamped down the gears. You can do that, or you can smoothly go 3..2..1. If you're aggressive, though, it upsets the suspension. Of course I turn the throttle as fast as I can, but that's never going to wear the bike out. Everyone says I'm so smooth, yet I feel on the limit all the time and as if I am sliding loads. However, even my mum says I look boring. Maybe it's because I don't hang off the bike to turn it. I lean across it like a dirt bike, put it onto my knee and keep the weight over the top.

When things are going really good, you are so inch perfect that everything seems in slow motion. I've actually occasionally thought the bike's slowing down. You go past the pits and see the lap time and think 'How have I done that?' When things are bad – as they were during these races – I've no feel for what's happening beneath me. It's as if I could crash at every corner, and it feels like I'm doing 260mph down the straights. That's a horrible feeling. Riding well is all about confidence. When I'm confident I can go into slow motion straight away. If I could control that feeling I would probably be world champion right now instead of Troy.

As it was, I had to be content to battle it out for the minor places. I caught Broc Parkes with three laps to go and knew that we would both be able to catch Chili. We did go past him at the start of the final lap and I lined up Parkes with three corners to go, to move into seventh. Laconi, who had been on it all weekend and had amazingly been unhurt in the crash with Bayliss, managed to pip Xaus for his first podium finish of the season. He was maybe another one to be worrying about his job for next year! On my warm-down lap I was thinking 'This has been a disastrous end to the season, but at least I passed two people on my final lap of the year.' Okay, I admit that's clutching at straws for consolation!

Not surprisingly, I wasn't in much of a mood for an end-of-season party. I was starving hungry and wolfed down two full pizzas when we nipped into the centre of Imola, which was just a few hundred metres from the circuit, for a meal with Darrell and Michelle, who needed to be back early for the gala SBK banquet and awards ceremony. By that stage, though, the beer was beginning to stick in my throat, and not just because I'd eaten too much. I went to the team hotel for a while for a chat with the lads and showed my face at the SBK event for 20 minutes. Jamie's band, The Po Boys, were also playing at the Castrol Honda hospitality, where there had been a big punch-up earlier in the evening and the police were called in when Suzuki tried to settle a dispute with Yamaha from the World Supersport race. But I felt the evening was dragging on, and while Kathryn and the others bopped away, I was happier having a few beers outside the tent with some mates from Burnley.

Back in bed by 12.30, it was inevitable that I found myself reflecting on the season with Flat Eric. I'm still improving as a rider and have learnt a lot this year. The team has also learnt a lot. There is no doubt that we will be a stronger package come March next year, because we know that the bike will be faster. We also know where some of the weaknesses are in the team – and how to improve them. I don't think we have used telemetry enough to help guide the riders with set-up. We only have four hours to set the bike up. Even when track conditions don't change those four hours soon go and we have tended to restrict the computer information to engine performance. In the cold light of day, we don't need the computer when we are riding round Donington Park and Brands Hatch. I'm sensitive to one click of rebound at those circuits. At tracks like this that I don't know, I'm not even sensitive to something major like an offset change. Sometimes I've felt rushed into making a decision, which means that everyone follows you down the wrong path. So there are rough edges to smooth off – we know that.

Hopefully there will not be as many breakdowns next year and there will definitely be a more comprehensive testing programme. I know that I will be a better rider and I also now know that I can beat the likes of Bayliss, Xaus, Bostrom and Edwards – as it will be those guys who are up there at the front again. The old Neil Hodgson might have been happy to come fifth in the World Superbike championship. The new Neil Hodgson isn't. And I truly believe that, this time next year, I will not just be back on track – I will be a world champion.

Round by Round Results

Valencia – round 1

Race 1	RET (crashed)
Race 2	5th

Kyalami – round 2

Race 1	RET (engine failure)
Race 2	4th

Phillip Island – round 3

Race 1	11th (remounted after crashing)
Race 2	Cancelled due to rain

Sugo – round 4

Race 1	7th
Race 2	5th

Monza – round 5

Race 1	RET (engine failure)
Race 2	7th

Donington – round 6

Race 1   1st
Race 2   2nd

EuroSpeedway Lausitz – round 7

Race 1   8th
Race 2   2nd

Misano – round 8

Race 1   6th
Race 2   16th (tyre problem)

Laguna Seca – round 9

Race 1   2nd
Race 2   3rd

Brands Hatch – round 10

Race 1   2nd
Race 2   2nd

Oscherleben – round 11

Race 1   7th
Race 2   10th

Assen – round 12

Race 1   5th
Race 2   5th

Imola– round 13

Race 1   10th
Race 2   7th

World Superbike Championships 2001 Final standings

Pos.	Rider	No.	Team	Points
1.	Troy Bayliss	21	Ducati Infostrada	369
2.	Colin Edwards	1	Castrol Honda	333
3.	Ben Bostrom	155	Ducati L&M	312
4.	Troy Corser	3	Virgilio Aprilla Axo	284
5.	Neil Hodgson	100	GSE Racing	269
6.	Ruben Xaus	11	Ducati Infostrada	236
7.	Pierfrancesco Chili	4	Suzuki Alstare Corona	232
8.	Tadayuki Okada	8	Castrol Honda	176
9.	Akira Yanagawa	5	Fuchs Kawasaki	170
10.	Gregorio Lavilla	6	Fuchs Kawasaki	166
11.	Regis Laconi	55	Virgilio Aprilia Axo	152
12.	Stephane Chambon	24	Suzuki Alstare Corona	122
13.	James Toseland	52	GSE Racing	91
14.	Hitoyasu Izutsu	19	Fuchs Kawasaki	63
15.	Makota Tamada	49	Cabin Honda	50

16.	Broc Parkes	36	Ducati NCR	49
17.	Steve Martin	99	DFX Racing	47
18.	Giovanni Bussei	35	Ducati NCR	44
19.	Lucio Pedercini	22	Pedercini	32
20.	Robert Ulm	33	Kawasaki Bertocchi	28
21.	Eric Bostrom	32	Kawasaki Motors C.	22
22.	Alessandro Antonello	30	Virgilio Aprilia Axo	21
23.	Alex Gramigni	39	Valli Moto 391	21
24.	Shinichi Ito	50	Cabin Honda	20
25.	John Reynolds	60	Revè Red Bull Ducati	20
26.	Akira Ryo	48	Suzuki	20
27.	Marco Borciani	20	Pedercini	17
28.	Steve Hislop	61	Monster Mob Ducati	16
29.	Tamaki Serizawa	54	Kawasaki Racing	16
30.	Mauro Sanchini	46	Pedercini	16
31.	Martin Craggill	51	Pacific	16
32.	Sean Emmett	62	Revè Red Bull Ducati	13
33.	Juan Bautista Borja	7	Panavto Yamaha	12
34.	Bertrand Stey	27	White Endurance	8
35.	Doug Chandler	10	Kawasaki Motors C.	7
36.	Peter Goddard	14	Benelli Sport	7
37.	Yukio Kagayama	56	Suzuki	6
38.	Wataru Yoshikawa	53	Yamaha Racing	6
39.	Alistair Maxwell	45	SRT Almax	3
40.	Michele Malatesta	31	Kawasaki Bertocchi	3
41.	Paolo Blora	113	DCR	2
42.	Ludovic Holon	41	Kawasaki Bertocchi	1
43.	Jiri Mrkyvka	23	JM SBK	1
44.	Javier Rodriguez	25	Ghelfi Art	1